THE MAKING
Rhodes

BBC Books

THE MAKING OF
Rhodes

Fliss Coombs

ACKNOWLEDGEMENTS
With thanks to: Lyn Avery, Frances Barber,
Adam Browne, Maurice Cain, Gerry Crampton, David Drury,
Oliver Fryer, Isobel Gillan, Heather Holden-Brown, Gavin
Hood, Pamela Joyce, Kate Lock, Scott Meek, Gavin Mey, Neil
Pearson, Ivan Rendall, Charles and Harriet Salmon, RoseAnn
Samuel, Amanda Sarosi, Joe Shaw, Martin Shaw, Nigel Stafford-
Clark, Archie Tait, Antony Thomas, Graham
Walker, John Watson and Doug Young

**And with special personal thanks to
Christopher Hansard and Siobhan Lyons**

Published by BBC Books,
an imprint of BBC Worldwide Publishing.
BBC Worldwide Limited, Woodlands,
80 Wood Lane, London W12 0TT

First published 1996
© Fliss Coombs, 1996
The moral right of the author has been asserted

ISBN 0 563 38785 8

Maps by Line and Line
All photographs Zenith Productions/BBC (Umberto Adaggi), except
the following: Gary Moyes 18, 26, 28, 30, 37, 39, 42, 43, 48, 52, 58,
70–71, 85 (top), 91; courtesy Antony Thomas 8, 27 (top); Lisa Trocchi
82; Frank Spooner 123; Tom Stoddart/PG 125.

Printed and bound in Great Britain by Butler & Tanner Ltd,
Frome and London
Colour separations by Radstock Reproductions Ltd, Midsomer
Norton
Cover printed by Clays Ltd, St Ives plc

Previous page: *Martin Shaw as Cecil Rhodes*

Contents

Introduction

Scott Meek, managing director of Zenith and producer of Rhodes

I first met Cecil Rhodes in 1984. I had just started work at Zenith Productions and had been a script editor for all of a week. I didn't really know what I was doing, so I was making it up as I went along. Twelve years later I've discovered that everyone makes it up as they go along. And that's because we're manufacturing dreams.

All dramas are someone's dream. It's almost always the writer's, but sometimes a producer or director is possessed by a story that must be told. When I first encountered the ghost of Cecil Rhodes through the scripts of Antony Thomas and the vision of Margaret Matheson, who had commissioned them, the telling of Rhodes's story was Antony's dream. All I knew about Rhodes was that he was something to do with Rhodesia and Rhodes scholars. Of his incalculable wealth, of his control of the world's diamonds, of his bullying and bribery, murder and extortion, I knew nothing. In the next 12 years I would learn about power, corruption, ruthless ambition and theft from Rhodes, and about grace, honour, consistency and vision from Antony.

By the time Rhodes had moved from scripts discussed around a kitchen table in Shepherd's Bush to a high plateau in South Africa, I had travelled via Antony's imagination not only to another continent, but to another century. This was not just a writer's dream, it was a revelation: a notion of empire totally different – and infinitely more compelling – than the one we had learned at school.

To tell the epic story of a charismatic, piratical figure who 'ate countries for breakfast' and not only provide hours of enthralling viewing but perhaps leave the audience understanding a little part of history better – well, to use Rhodes's words, 'What a dream!'. This fabulous combination of J.R. Ewing filtered through H. Rider Haggard and Machiavelli kept us going for years and years. Rhodes had gripped our imagination and, true to the old bugger's manipulative spirit, wouldn't let go.

Many projects simply have to wait until they find their moment. *Rhodes* became viable when the new South Africa began to emerge in 1990. A team of people who had stuck with the project from its early stages were still involved: Maurice Cain, production designer on the series for over 10 years; Michael Wearing and Kate Harwood of the BBC, whose admiration of the scripts had been unwavering; Charles Denton, whose support as managing director of Zenith and later as head of drama for BBC Television, remained constant; Nigel Stafford-Clark, to whom I am eternally grateful for reducing the scripts from 11½ hours to nine without losing the sense or integrity of the series; Chris Catterall, Fliss Coombs and Dorothy Berwin of Zenith, and many, many more.

We were joined by others whose enthusiasm was matched only by their exceptional talents. David Drury, a director mad enough to imagine that he could carry the detail of nine hours of story in his head, shot out of sequence, while commanding an army and working seven days a week for the best part of a year (the six-month shoot was just the beginning – he spent many more months in post-production). Charles Salmon, a producer who never panics, even when he's confronted by several miles of 15-feet-high flames racing towards an irreplaceable set. And Martin Shaw, who quite simply became Rhodes – but, thankfully, returned to being himself whenever the camera stopped turning.

My lasting impressions are of thousands of people, a dozen years of preparation, a great vision, the African sun, the high veld, waggon trains, fires, Zulu battles, camp fires, cold beer and camaraderie and the new Republic of South Africa. It was the adventure of a lifetime. To everyone involved, thank you. And to everyone who watches and enjoys *Rhodes*, this is the story of how it was done.

SCOTT MEEK

On location in
South Africa

Chapter 1

The Extraordinary Life of Cecil Rhodes

Cecil Rhodes
c. 1897

Cecil John Rhodes was born on 5 July 1853 in Bishop's Stortford, England, the fourth surviving son of a country parson, one of a family of nine children. A sickly child, he attended the village school, unlike his three elder brothers who were educated at Eton and Winchester. Yet, by the time he was 45, he was one of the wealthiest men in the Western world with 440 000 square miles of southern Africa named after him.

In 1870, the delicate 17-year-old joined his brother, Herbert, and thousands of adventurers and outlaws in the frenzied rush for diamonds in the South African veld. The young Cecil Rhodes soon revealed an astute business sense, securing pumping monopolies on the Dutoitspan and De Beers mines and establishing the main source of the diamonds. By the age of 20 he had suffered his first heart attack and returned to England to study at the University of Oxford. It was here that a burning ambition began to grip his imagination. He deduced that God was perfecting the human race through natural selection and that, in his opinion, the people that God had most brought to flower were the English-speaking race – the people of Great Britain, her dominions and America. He contended that the more the world was inhabited by the English, the better it would be and decided that he would work for the furtherance of the British Empire. He would secure Africa – and diamonds would give him the means to achieve that end.

Back in Kimberley in Cape Colony (now Cape Province), the heart of the diamond-mining country, he expanded his business operations ruthlessly, eliminating rivals with his brilliant schemes. He amalgamated a large number of diamond-mining claims to form the De Beers Mining Company and in 1881 he gained a powerful foothold in the Cape Parliament. He outwitted his greatest rival, the colourful Barney Barnato, thus gaining a virtual monopoly of the world's diamonds. He would stop at nothing to achieve his ultimate goal – to seize as much of 'unclaimed Africa' as he could lay his hands on.

He set his sights on the riches of Matabeleland and Mashonaland, territories occupied by a mighty Zulu army, the Matabele, and his agents tricked their king, Lobengula, into signing a document endorsed by Queen Victoria which granted Rhodes exclusive mineral rights to the region. But his scheme misfired badly.

Lobengula sent a deputation to the Queen who confirmed that she had authorized no such document. Back in England, Rhodes worked feverishly to repair the damage, bribing politicians and newspaper proprietors and influencing all shades of opinion using a combination of oratory, flattery and wealth. After six months of hard lobbying, he received parliamentary approval for a royal charter and, too late, Lobengula realized that he had signed over his kingdom to Cecil Rhodes.

Banned by the high commissioner of the Cape from taking Matabeleland from the angry Lobengula by force, the relentless Rhodes ordered his most trusted accomplice, Dr Leander Starr Jameson, to lead an army of so-called 'pioneers' recruited by a young mercenary soldier, Frank Johnson, to take neighbouring Mashonaland instead. The African continent – or so it seemed – was ready to fall into his grasp. Rhodes's vision was of a great new country, more powerful and more populous than the United States of America.

But the dream was short-lived. Mashonaland was not laden with the promised gold and Rhodes's company was on the verge of collapse. He had to take Matabeleland, using whatever devious means possible. Jameson was put in charge and provoked a border incident, allowing Rhodes to invade in the name of 'self-defence'. Three thousand Matabele warriors were slaughtered on the battlefields and the defeated Lobengula escaped into the veld to commit ritual suicide.

With the granting of the royal charter in 1889, Rhodes's influential British South Africa Company (known as the Chartered Company) governed what are today Zimbabwe and Zambia up until 1923. In 1890, he became prime minister of Cape Colony. Triumphantly, he told his shareholders in London that they owned 'a very large piece of the world'. Four years later in 1894, the 440 000 square miles of Matabeleland, Mashonaland Manica, Barotseland and other territories were united and named 'Rhodesia' in his honour. (By the time of his death, Rhodes had brought almost a million square miles of the continent under British domination.)

In a stirring speech to the Cape Parliament, Rhodes laid down the principles of what later became apartheid, seeking to end black self-sufficiency by confining rural Africans to limited tribal areas and imposing a tax of 10 s on every hut. To survive, Africans would have to sell their labour to whites. His proposals became law. But his attempt to take the gold-rich Transvaal ended in defeat and humiliation

RHODES

when he secretly conspired to overthrow the Boer-dominated Transvaal Government. A revolt in Johannesburg was to be provoked and privately supported by Dr Jameson, now British administrator of the lands constituting present-day Zimbabwe. But on 29 December 1895, Jameson invaded the Transvaal prematurely and unsuccessfully. Rhodes was censured for his role in what became known as 'the Jameson Raid' and was forced to resign his premiership.

Rhodes then devoted himself to the development of Rhodesia, but the Shona and the Matabele united and rose against him in bloody rebellion. In the noblest moment of his life, Rhodes walked unarmed onto the battlefield to plead for peace, and the Matabele laid down their guns.

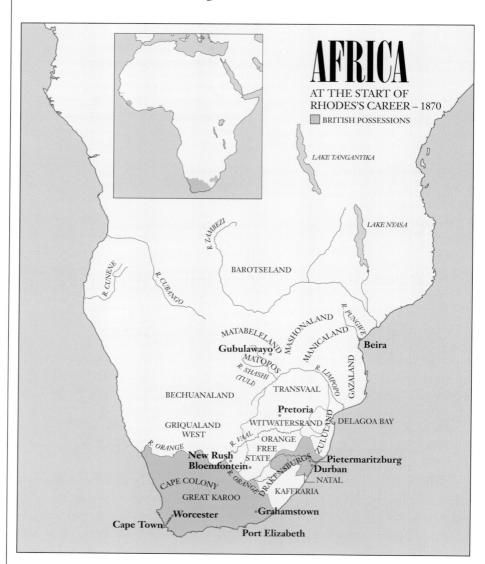

AFRICA
AT THE START OF
RHODES'S CAREER – 1870
BRITISH POSSESSIONS

LAKE TANGANYIKA

LAKE NYASA

R. ZAMBEZI

R. CUNENE

R. CUBANGO

BAROTSELAND

R. PUNGWE

MATABELELAND

MASHONALAND

MANICALAND

Gubulawayo

Beira

MATOPOS

R. SHASHI (TULI)

GAZALAND

R. LIMPOPO

BECHUANALAND

TRANSVAAL

Pretoria

GRIQUALAND WEST

WITWATERSRAND

DELAGOA BAY

ZULULAND

R. ORANGE

R. VAAL

ORANGE FREE STATE

New Rush

Bloemfontein

DRAKENSBURGS

Pietermaritzburg

R. ORANGE

Durban

NATAL

CAPE COLONY

KAFERARIA

GREAT KAROO

Worcester

Grahamstown

Cape Town

Port Elizabeth

The fuse in the Transvaal had been lit and within four years it exploded into the Boer War. Now Rhodes faced his greatest enemy — the woman who set out to conquer him. Princess Radziwill investigated the dark secrets of his rise to power in an attempt to blackmail him into marriage.

The princess literally hounded the ailing Rhodes to death. He died in Cape Town in March 1902, two months before the end of the Boer War, and was buried in the Matopos hills in Rhodesia, his country. As his coffin was lowered into the ground, thousands of Matabele warriors swarmed over the granite hillside. The voices of the Africans he had won, betrayed and won over again were united in one cry, 'Bayete!'. He is the only white man in history to have received the Zulu royal salute.

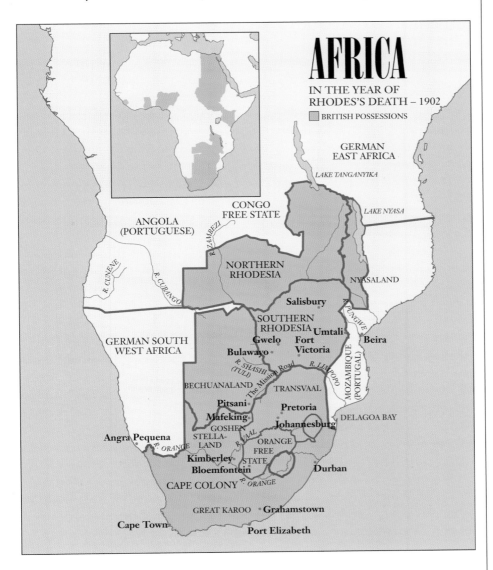

Chapter 2

Twelve years of struggle

The creator and writer of *Rhodes*, Antony Thomas, has written, directed and produced television documentaries and dramas that have won him international acclaim and numerous awards, including two of the most prestigious – the international Emmy and the British Academy Award. His documentary trilogy *The South African Experience* was seen in 35 countries and his drama *Death of a Princess* received the highest ratings in the history of public television when it was shown in the United States.

As a young boy growing up with his grandparents in South Africa, Antony Thomas was regularly taken to see the statue of Cecil Rhodes in the botanical gardens near the Cape Town Parliament, which depicts him pointing north across the Dark Continent.

'To my grandparents, Rhodes was a symbol of everything that was fine about their tradition and everything that was noble about being British. He justified our presence in that part of Africa. He represented everything we aspired to – he defined who we were. I was taught to thank God every night in my prayers for making me English.'

Born in Calcutta in 1940, Antony Thomas was taken to live in South Africa when he was six years old. Despite his conservative upbringing, by his mid-20s he was a political activist, committed to the campaign for a non-racial South Africa. He supported the African National Congress in its armed struggle against apartheid and left South Africa for England in 1967, unable to tolerate the regime's interference in his film-making activities.

His interest in Rhodes was first awakened in 1970 when he was asked by actor/writer Kenneth Griffith to direct one of his personal documentaries on the British imperialist. Rhodes emerged as a man who had commandeered a fortune in the no-holds-barred melee of the Kimberley diamond rush, and then used that fortune to murder, steal, bribe, cheat and corrupt, in a headlong rush to secure as much of Africa's land and mineral wealth as he could lay his hands on.

Opposite:
Martin Shaw as
Cecil Rhodes
in 1896

'Making that documentary was a painful experience for me,' says Thomas. 'It took me back to my childhood and filled me with a sense of self-disgust because Rhodes was part of my own identity.'

What started as a professional interest soon developed into a voracious appetite for more information. 'The weeks and months I spent studying biographies, letters, speeches, diaries and articles became a descent into evil. As the evidence accumulated, the man took a stronger and stronger hold on me. I found myself marvelling at his powers of persuasion, his extraordinary ability to achieve practically anything he wanted. I was stunned by his brilliance, by his sheer audacity. I even began to feel the pain of his emotional and personal life.'

Thomas was shocked by the extent to which Rhodes had contributed to the political evolution of South Africa. 'My grandparents had always told me that Rhodes was a 'father to the natives'. Like many English-speaking South Africans, they believed in the essential humanity of the English tradition, and that it was this sense of justice and decency that set us apart from the Afrikaners, who were turning their country into an international pariah.'

He soon learned, however, that if anyone could be accused of being the architect of apartheid, it was Cecil John Rhodes. In 1887, 61 years before the Nationalists came to power, Rhodes declared: 'These are my politics on native affairs, and these are the politics of South Africa…The native is to be treated as a child and denied the franchise…We must adopt a system of despotism, such as works so well in India, in our relations with the barbarians of South Africa.'

While recognizing that Rhodes needed to be viewed in the context of his time – an age when imperialism was akin to a religious ideal – as Thomas delved deeper into the mind and deeds of the man he uncovered a strikingly contemporary operator.

'His methods were very modern. He achieved a near-monopoly of the world's diamonds by manipulating the money markets, by audacious takeovers and by the secret purchase of shares. He had an innate understanding of public relations and of the power of the press. He acquired newspapers in the belief that 'the press rules the minds of men' and he knew that politicians and journalists could be bought with flattery and a few hundred pounds. He believed that every man had his price.'

Thomas was particularly moved by a collection of letters the 17-year-old Rhodes had written to his family when he first arrived in South Africa. They revealed a young man with an intuitive affinity for Africa and her people who enjoyed unusually relaxed relationships with local Africans and understood and appreciated their values. He was sensitive and perceptive, with an overriding sense of fairness and justice. Yet this was the boy who grew up to seize close on a million square miles of Africa, declaring, 'I prefer land to niggers'.

It became clear to Antony Thomas that Rhodes's progress from young diamond prospector to 'African Colossus' had the elements of classical tragedy – the tragedy of a young man's corruption in pursuit of power.

'I couldn't believe that this man who had made such a huge impact on Britain and Africa had been so easily – or so conveniently – forgotten. It was monstrous to ignore him. Then I had a mad thought. Might it be possible to bring the story of Cecil Rhodes to a mass audience through the medium of television?'

The lunacy of this thought soon became apparent to Antony and to everyone with whom he discussed it. 'Firstly there was the scale of his life. It wasn't possible to condense it into four or six hours, which is the standard requirement for a TV drama series these days. Huge sets would be essential, beginning with the re-creation of Kimberley and the diamond mines. Extras would be needed by the thousand, as would whole cavalries and regiments of warriors, along with ox-waggons, horsedrawn carriages, stage-coaches and at least two nineteenth-century trains. Above all, the series needed Africa – its people, its light, its landscape.'

Undaunted, he began writing, and in 1983 took his long-cherished dream to the newly formed independent production company Zenith, headed at that time by Charles Denton (who had supported him as a documentary-maker in the days of ATV) and Margaret Matheson. They supported the project wholeheartedly, as did Scott Meek, but the subject was still extremely sensitive. The obstacles to shooting the series in South Africa – the only feasible location – seemed to be insuperable. The struggle against apartheid had become increasingly violent, Nelson Mandela was still behind bars and international pressure on P.W. Botha's regime was intensifying. South Africa was still out of bounds, economically, culturally and politically isolated from the rest of the world.

The series' writer and creator, Antony Thomas, on location with Martin Shaw

By 1990, economic and diplomatic pressures, rising violence, falling white living standards and President F.W. de Klerk's own change of heart all combined to instigate change. The release of Nelson Mandela demonstrated that the world's last racial oligarchy was coming to an end.

The African National Congress, which had strongly supported the project from the outset, agreed that the script 'got to the roots of the long history of exploitation and dispossession of South Africa', and in 1990, after years of negotiation and diplomacy, the white government said it had no objection to the series being made on home ground.

Once again, the project came back to life. Scott Meek, by now head of Zenith, secured the BBC's interest in 1994 and serious consideration was given to the viability of production.

If *Rhodes* were to be shot entirely on location in South Africa and ready for transmission in autumn 1996, the six-month shoot had to start in May 1995 to take advantage of four months' guaranteed fine weather before the rainy season.

In 1994, Scott Meek took the decision to hire producer Charles Salmon, in the firm belief that the series would be made. Salmon and his production designer, Maurice Cain, carried out extensive location searches ('recces') in South Africa with Antony Thomas, working on the premise that filming would begin in May 1995. South Africa's winter months from May to September are always dry and sunny with clear blue skies from dawn to dusk, a film producer's dream: weather is always the great unknown quantity which can have a devastating effect on the schedule and budget. By October, the scorching heat is intolerable and the rainy season sets in, bringing daily thunderstorms that turn the dusty open veld (South African grassland) into a sea of mud. 'When we were looking for locations in November, if you put your arm out of the car window you could literally smell your skin burning within minutes,' recalls Salmon.

Martin Shaw, having first been approached about playing Rhodes 10 years before, confirmed his commitment to the project and casting the other lead parts began in earnest – although at that point there was still no guarantee that the series would go ahead. Director David Drury was signed up and joined Charles Salmon and Maurice Cain at the provisional base in South Africa. Meanwhile, Scott Meek had one further problem – would the massive budget of £10 m be agreed in time?

It was not until the middle of February, when day after precious day was passing, that he received the news he'd been hoping for since the day Antony Thomas first broached the project, 12 years before. The BBC, in partnership with the Canadian Broadcasting Company (CBC), confirmed that they were giving the production the green light.

Scott Meek and the team that had remained committed to the project for so many years always wondered how they would feel if they eventually heard this news. 'If we ever make *Rhodes…*' had been part of their vocabulary since its inception. 'I thought we'd be whooping for joy, dancing in the streets, cracking open champagne,' Meek says. 'Instead we just stood in stunned silence. I don't think we really believed it. Everyone just kept saying, "You mean we're actually going to do it?".'

Setting up in South Africa

Once reality had sunk in, the matter of the budget became critical. For film and television producers, the budget is the one overriding factor that dominates all creative and practical matters. The feasibility of any project depends on meticulously calculated figures. To arrive at these totals, the producer works closely with the production designer to ascertain whether the creative demands of the production and the budget are compatible. The biggest cost on most productions is manpower. The cast and crew amount to an enormous army of people and costs escalate dramatically if they have to be moved from place to place. Finding locations within a viable distance from one central base is therefore the crucial factor that can dictate whether or not a production goes ahead.

In *Rhodes*, the principal locations in real life are hundreds of miles apart. In any case, they now bear no resemblance to how they looked at the end of the last century and some no longer exist. Charles Salmon and Maurice Cain had to decide which real locations could be adapted and used for filming and what sets could be built from scratch in the same area. They had the whole of South Africa to consider. But where to start?

It would have been an insurmountable problem, had it not been for Antony Thomas's discovery of a vast area of private land only 40 minutes' drive from Johannesburg on a previous recce several months before. Nash's Farm had everything the producers needed: hundreds of square miles of varied African landscape; open veld as far as the eye could see; rolling hills; wooded valleys and miles of dirt tracks. In addition, the farm had a large existing stable block for housing and training the many horses that would be used throughout the production.

The discovery and availability of this land made the whole production financially viable. Existing locations in Johannesburg and Pretoria were within reach and the principal sets could all be accommodated somewhere on Nash's Farm.

On the nearest main road to Nash's Farm a small disused shopping complex and Zenex petrol station proved to be a perfect production base. The empty premises provided offices and space to accommodate hundreds of costumes, workrooms for the wardrobe and art departments, and a large car park and forecourt for the massive transport department.

Zenex became the nerve centre of the whole production and, early in 1995, large areas of Nash's Farm started to undergo dramatic transformation under the watchful eye of Maurice Cain. They had three months. Shooting was due to begin on 29 May.

Rhodes *is the end result of years of dedication and exhaustive research on the part of Antony Thomas. His list of reference sources alone runs to 78 pages and includes extracts from private letters, unpublished manuscripts and diaries as well as transcripts of interviews with African witnesses. Much of the series is based on verbatim accounts provided by people who were there on the spot and of the two hundred or so characters in the series, only one is fictional.*

In episodes four and eight, Thomas can be seen playing the radical Liberal MP La Bouchère who opposed Rhodes's application for a royal charter and later took him to task during the parliamentary enquiry into the disastrous Jameson Raid.

Chapter 3

Working in South Africa

Third assistant director, Philip Mosoeu

Filming an epic drama in a country so new to freedom had its problems. South Africa's history of racial segregation and isolation from the rest of the world and the conflict, hatred and deprivation that marks its recent past (and still exists) is such that people are suspicious of further exploitation. On the practical side, the extremes of wealth and poverty have produced a country that is a curious mix of Western sophistication and Third World underdevelopment and inefficiency.

South Africa's film industry is relatively new to the world of international co-productions and has limited experience of projects made on the scale of *Rhodes*. Charles Salmon and his South African production supervisor Pierre de Hinch decided, therefore, to hire British heads of departments, who, in turn, hired their own South African technicians. The producers were keen to hire a racially mixed crew but the employment of black South Africans was inevitably restricted by the lack of training opportunities during the years of apartheid. Drivers, cooks, seamstresses and manual workers were hired from the townships of Alexandria and Soweto and it was hoped that the hiring of several young black assistants and trainees would help to sow the seeds of a more integrated film industry in the future. Nonetheless, it was potentially a politically sensitive mix that might have smacked of the days of British colonialism that the series was about to re-create.

One of the first hurdles that had to be overcome was the mistrust that South African unions, technicians and actors have towards foreign production companies. In the 1980s, when most mainstream film companies were still boycotting the country, many less scrupulous producers were attracted by financial advantages

18

rather than the locations, skills and resources of the local film industry. 'People are still deeply suspicious of the views and perceptions of the outside world,' acknowledges Charles Salmon.

The pre-production period involved protracted and difficult negotiations with the unions and the Consultative Committee, a non-governmental arbitration authority that was initially wary of allowing a British cast and crew to work in the country. The onus was on *Rhodes*'s producers to convince them of the integrity of the project and to prove that, far from exploiting their members, they had much to offer them in terms of gaining experience and expertise.

However, it was an uphill struggle. With only weeks to go before the start of shooting at the end of May, the authorities were still refusing to grant work permits for several key positions, including the stunt co-ordinator and the special effects supervisor. Temporary visas had to be obtained and several British crew members flew out to South Africa not knowing whether they would have to return within a few weeks or whether they would be able to stay for the whole six months.

It took enormous patience and diplomacy to secure work permits for every British employee, but in the end Charles Salmon succeeded. 'We did finally manage to win round the unions and the Consultative Committee and after a while, they were positively co-operative.'

Director David Drury with Ramolao Makhene (Babayane) and Ken Gampu (Mshete), the two indunas *who visit Queen Victoria in England*

Practicalities

Obtaining the work permits was the first step. Entering the country was the next. Despite the fact that South Africa is now 'open for business' to the rest of the world, the immigration authorities at Johannesburg Airport were less than welcoming. New arrivals were subjected to delays and close questioning about the nature of their visit, despite having the necessary documentation, and director David Drury was held in a cell and questioned for four hours before he could enter the country.

The telephone, lifeline of any production and taken for granted in any modern capital city, became a permanent headache for the production team. It can take months for a phone line to be installed, then a thunderstorm can cause the whole system to go down. Cut telephone wires are also unfortunately a regular feature of crime-ridden Johannesburg, where they're turned into copper bracelets and sold to tourists as ethnic jewellery. On one occasion, the production office was out of communication for several days because the entire local telephone exchange had been stolen.

Settling in

The British crew had to adjust quickly to day-to-day life and attitudes in South Africa, and some of their first experiences had not been promising. Democracy, after all, was only one year old and South African society is still deeply divided. A large party seemed the ideal way to launch the production – a chance for the huge cast and crew to meet and get to know each other. The practical and political problems, however, were overwhelming. A suitable location was found near the production base, north of Johannesburg, but this proved to be too far away from the townships where the black crew members lived. In any case, it was considered undiplomatic to hold the party in a white area, even with transport provided to and from the townships. An alternative location in downtown Johannesburg was suggested, but few whites would consider venturing into such an unsafe area after dark. In the end, the proposition was reluctantly abandoned. (It is a tribute to the spirit of the production and of the new South Africa that no such problems prevented the end-of-shoot party being one that every member of the crew attended and celebrated wholeheartedly.)

As the British crew members were spending more than six months on location it made sense for them to rent accommodation, rather than staying in hotels. The houses they rented in leafy suburbia were staffed by black servants whose living and employment conditions often belied the ideals of the post-apartheid South Africa. A black housekeeper who was given a wedding present by Charles Salmon took three days to summon up the courage to come and thank him, explaining that he had never received such kindness from a white person before and that he was 'more frightened of white people than lions'.

In Johannesburg, violent crime is a feature of everyday life and shootings and carjackings are as common a topic of conversation as the weather is in England. For all that, South Africa is changing — and that spirit was never more evident than during the 1995 Rugby World Cup, which took place during filming and captured the imagination of the entire nation. The cast and crew celebrated South Africa's win on the streets of Johannesburg where, for once, its population was united by a new sense of national pride.

Different ways of working

South Africa is a country with no less than 11 official languages and only nine per cent of the population speaks English as a mother tongue. Many South Africans are bilingual or even trilingual, speaking English, Afrikaans and Zulu (the latter is spoken by 22 per cent of the people). Although the production was English-speaking, negotiations were often conducted in Afrikaans and Zulu speakers were essential to co-ordinate scenes requiring extras.

Communications complications aside, even experienced members of the South African film crew were unused to the rigorous demands of working on a British production, which is run along the lines of a military operation. Lost minutes represent lost money, and to avoid that everything is planned down to the last detail. This sort of discipline was new to the South Africans and caused a few problems in the early days. Crew members were late, drivers got lost, essential

Director David Drury and Maureen Conway, in charge of continuity, with one of the Matabele warriors

vehicles were in the wrong place at the wrong time and, because most of the drivers lived in the townships where telephones are a luxury, it was impossible to contact them to find out where they were.

'We had a few teething problems because they weren't used to productions on this scale. Things tended to take longer than they should and the logistics presented enormous problems,' says director David Drury. Example rather than conflict proved to be the solution. 'We adapted and so did they,' Drury continues. 'Despite bushfires, dust storms, thousands of extras to co-ordinate, hundreds of horses, battle sequences and filming in remote areas where there was no communication with the office, we finished bang on schedule.'

'The majority of the South African crew saw the production as an opportunity to learn,' adds Charles Salmon. 'Equally, the British crew had to adapt to working in a difficult environment with different priorities, so it was definitely a two-way process.'

By the end of the shoot Scott Meek was delighted with the way the British and South Africans had pulled together. 'The spirit on the production was tremendous. Some crew members were more experienced than others and many had to learn on the job, but, at the end of the day, the commitment to the work and the energy was fantastic. When I saw how constructively black and white South Africans were working together I thought, Yes, it is possible to have a functioning multi-racial society here. And when people in South Africa see the show they should feel proud to know that it is 90 per cent made by South Africans.'

Sean Taylor plays Frank Thompson, the former compound manager of De Beers who became Rhodes's principal agent in Matabeleland

CASTING

Finding and securing the right actor for each part is the job of the casting director. Final decisions rest creatively with the director and financially with the producer, but the casting director puts forward suggestions and negotiates with actors' agents on behalf of the production. Because casting is based on personal knowledge and experience, a local casting director is essential when overseas actors are required for a foreign location.

There are 198 speaking parts in the series, only 13 of which were to be played by British actors. In England, casting director Sarah Bird concentrated on finding suitable actors for those roles, while her counterpart in South Africa, Christa Schamburger, had the daunting task of finding the remaining 185.

While director David Drury was in England working on the scripts, Schamburger held casting sessions with South African actors, which she recorded on video. The tapes were sent to him to make shortlists which would be followed up when he returned to Johannesburg.

David Drury had to meet each South African actor to decide if they were right for the part, but the interviews worked both ways: they wanted to meet him to check that the subject would be dealt with honestly. The director had to convince them that the series would neither adulate nor denigrate Rhodes, but simply attempt to tell the truth.

The producers were particularly worried that black actors might be reluctant to take part, given the sensitivity of the subject – Rhodes was, after all, responsible for initiating racial segregation. However, once the potential cast read through their parts, which were in the Ndebele (Matabele) language, word went out that this was a refreshingly bold and honest production. Top black actors joined the cast, including Patrick Shai as Christmas and the award-winning actor and musician Washington Sixolo as Matabele chief Lobengula.

Washington Sixolo had good reason to trust the integrity of the series. When David Drury first met him to talk about the part, he was surprised to find that the imposing actor had brought an even larger friend with him, who listened in brooding silence as Drury talked about Lobengula and his court at Gubulawayo. 'I became increasingly uncomfortable as I spoke, aware that I hadn't researched the subject thoroughly and that I might unwittingly be making some political gaffes. Who was I to be telling them about their own history?'

Finally, Sixolo's anonymous friend said, 'It was so. That was what happened.' Only then did Drury learn that he was actually Lobengula's great-grandson. For Sixolo, the family's confirmation of the facts was the seal of approval: 'This series will be an education to a lot of people who are going to learn how black people were exploited. It will be an eye-opener to the people of South Africa.'

*Producer
Charles Salmon
visits the set*

Chapter 4

Creating Rhodes's World

Maurice Cain, the production designer on *Rhodes*, is one of only three members of the team who was involved in the series from the very outset. As head of the art department he was responsible for overseeing virtually everything on screen that doesn't move, from adapting real locations to designing and building sets and selecting and supplying all the props.

While his initial research continued to stand him in good stead, the project went through many different phases over the 12 years of planning and waiting, and Cain had to adjust his ideas accordingly. 'Originally, we were thinking of filming in the actual locations in England and South Africa, but this simply wasn't viable because of cost and practical problems. We soon realized that, for financial reasons, we would have to shoot everything in South Africa,' he explains. 'It was only when we discovered Nash's Farm that we started to think in terms of building our own major sets and adapting locations, so that we could keep the same production base.'

Building individual sets is a common practice in the world of television and film-making. But building entire towns and communities made up of real buildings and not facades is virtually unknown since the early days of Hollywood. Nevertheless, this was Maurice Cain's challenge for *Rhodes*.

Before construction of the sets began, he created them painstakingly in miniature, making models that replicated the final sets in every detail. There were seven major sites, the most ambitious being the town of Kimberley and Lobengula's kraal at Gubulawayo, and the others making up New Rush/Kimberley mine, Fort Victoria, the De Beers compound, Ferrieras camp and Fort Salisbury. In addition, Cain and his team built a further 28 smaller sets and adapted 36 locations.

Kimberley

The shanty town that initially grew up alongside the diamond diggings near the Vaal river was, appropriately, called New Rush. In 1873 it was annexed by the British, who considered its original epithet somewhat vulgar and renamed it Kimberley.

Opposite: The early diamond diggings of New Rush, later renamed Kimberley, one of the principal sets built on Nash's Farm

When Anthony Trollope first saw Kimberley in 1876 he said that he could not imagine an uglier place. There had been no rain for months. There wasn't a tree within five miles, the houses were all made of corrugated iron, there were no pavements and the roadways were just dust and holes. 'I seemed to breathe dust rather than air ... I was soon sick of looking at diamonds,' he wrote.

This was the town that Maurice Cain had to re-create, starting from bare, rock-laden earth in the middle of Nash's Farm. As ever, creativity was bound by a multitude of practical considerations. When he was choosing the exact site for Kimberley from hundreds of square miles of open country, he had to consider how well the surrounding landscape would photograph, where the sun set and whether the site would be accessible for the army of vehicles needed to support the production.

Production designer Maurice Cain built miniature models of all the sets he was to construct on Nash's Farm

As his starting point, Maurice Cain had made detailed studies of contemporary descriptions, old photographs and drawings, and then matched them to the needs of the script. His version of Kimberley consisted of 48 buildings and some 130 tents. It took 10 weeks to build, starting with earth-moving diggers in the open veld.

The series covers a period of 30 years, during which time Kimberley developed from a shanty town whose occupants lived in tents to a thriving, permanent community, which fell under the Boer siege in 1900. Just as the actors had to age according to which part of the story was being filmed, so did Kimberley. The London Hotel, the low-life dive for diggers, speculators and prostitutes, became the Barnato Mining Company building, corrugated shacks turned into shops and the tented encampments gradually gave way to small buildings as the town became more prosperous. The only brick building, the exclusive Kimberley Club, which was founded by Rhodes in 1880, was built on the edge of town once filming was under way. It was on the verandah of the Kimberley Club that Rhodes received General French, who relieved the town from the four-month siege at the start of the Boer War.

Although the corrugated-iron houses of Kimberley look basic, they were all designed and built by Maurice Cain as practical, functional buildings. Rhodes's house was a good example. Sir James Rose-Innes, later Chief Justice of the Union, described Rhodes's house in the year that he entered parliament as, 'A corrugated-iron shanty. Soiled and tumbled bed-clothes on an iron bed with a Gladstone bag for a bolster.' This was how the man who had just floated a company for £200,000 a year chose to live and the description provided invaluable detail and insight for Maurice Cain and his art department.

Because filming is scheduled around locations rather than the chronology of the story, every scene set at Kimberley was blocked together and filmed at the start of production over a period of several weeks. While interior scenes were being shot, the exteriors were prepared for the following day. Buildings were changed or aged for continuity purposes, flags raised or lowered, props brought in, carriages put in place, a diamond-buyer's shack converted into a vegetable shop and so on, depending on the requirements and the date of the scene being shot next. The final scenes shot at Kimberley were those that take place during the Boer War at the end of the series. Maurice Cain watched in quiet contemplation as his set was blown to smithereens by the Boer onslaught, courtesy of the special effects department.

The site for Kimberley was about two miles from the main road, up a dirt track. This track had to accommodate camera and lighting trucks, coaches full of extras, caravans for the actors, catering waggons, make-up and wardrobe buses,

The tented encampment above Kimberley which was devastated by a massive bushfire six weeks into the shoot (see pages 72–75)

portable toilets for the cast and crew, trucks full of livestock, and numerous period waggons, carts and carriages, as well as horses, which were ridden up by grooms and riders from the production's stables. The rocky track was hazardous and, despite stringent speed restrictions, numerous vehicles came to grief or got stuck and held up the whole convoy, wheels spinning hopelessly in the red dust.

Dust is the most distinctive feature of the high veld, the open grassland area north of Johannesburg where the series was filmed. Red dust fills the air, invades the nostrils and permeates everything. But it didn't satisfy Maurice Cain. 'Nature is never quite enough for the camera, that's why we use rain machines even when it's actually raining. To make sure that the dust really registered on screen, we covered the whole area with hundreds of tons of Fuller's Earth, which was mixed with powdered terracotta to give the dust its distinctive red colour.'

The dust was a constant nightmare for the camera crew, whose equipment needs to be kept scrupulously clean to avoid damage to the film, but it turned out to be a blessing for the wardrobe assistants, who were delighted that the costumes were convincingly filthy in no time at all. 'Normally we would have had to work very hard to achieve that effect,' explains costume designer Lyn Avery. 'For once we encouraged the actors to get their costumes as dirty as they liked!'

Lobengula's kraal

'Kraal' is the South African word for a native village. The kraal of Lobengula, king of the awesome Matabele, was at Gubulawayo, now Bulawayo, the second largest city in what became Rhodesia and is now Zimbabwe.

In real life, Bulawayo is over 1000 miles north of Kimberley. On Nash's Farm, the two sets were only a couple of miles apart. Building the kraal was probably Maurice Cain's greatest creative challenge. He knew from historical descriptions that it would have consisted of a group of traditional Zulu grass huts surrounded by an impenetrable wooden stockade. Within the kraal there was a further enclosure, the home of Lobengula, who was known as 'the Mighty Elephant'. Approaching his quarters would have involved crossing a ditch full of mud. This was not for protection, but the point at which anyone approaching had to prostrate themselves by crawling on their belly. No-one in the kraal was permitted to be higher than the king.

Likewise, the king's house would have been higher than any other building, with a raised platform outside from which he could address his *indunas*, or tribal councillors. There would also have been an open area for *indabas* (tribal conferences) to be held. These were Maurice Cain's guidelines, beyond which he had complete creative freedom.

The building of the kraal started, in effect, a year before Scott Meek received the go-ahead for the series. 'In the summer of 1994 we were still desperately fine-tuning the budget and the script in the hope that one day we would be able to make

*Part of
Lobengula's kraal,
built on Nash's
Farm by a team of
Zulu workers and
their families*

the series,' he says. 'We had location scouts and a production manager on board in South Africa so that we'd be prepared if we ever got the green light. One day I had a phone call from South Africa, explaining that, if the series were to be made in 1995, the grass for the Zulu huts in the kraal would have to be harvested there and then. It's special thatching grass from Zululand in Natal. I took a deep breath and ordered the grass to be harvested and stored. It seemed extraordinary to be making such a decision from my desk in London's West End – and even more extraordinary to see the end result almost a year later.'

A team of Zulu craftsmen and their families was recruited from Zululand to build the huts in the traditional way by weaving and plaiting the grass together over an intricate wooden frame. Each one took several weeks to complete and, as the huts took shape, the families moved into them. Such huts are still used by Zulus in Natal and provide more comfortable living conditions than the corrugated shacks that make up the townships. They maintain the same temperature inside regardless of the temperature outside, protecting the inhabitants from both the intense summer heat and the sub-zero African winter nights.

One of the highlights of the production was the completion of the kraal in July 1995. The Zulu workers threw an impromptu barbecue and invited the production and design teams to celebrate their fine work. A bonfire was lit under the stars and hunks of raw meat were thrown onto the fire and retrieved on the ends of sticks. A magnificent display of Zulu singing and dancing followed and speeches of thanks were made, translated and applauded, the women ululating their approval, the men growling theirs.

The only sadness was the knowledge that Rhodes's 'pioneer' army ultimately sacked Gubulawayo and razed it to the ground. Within weeks of completing the kraal, the set would be nothing but smouldering ruins...

From Windsor Castle to the Orange river

Suitable locations for scenes that take place in England also had to be found within striking distance of Nash's Farm, including an Oxford college and Oxford's Sheldonian Theatre, Windsor Castle, a London hotel, Ampney Park (the stately home of Lord Gifford), Cannon Street Hall in London and various rooms in the Palace of Westminster.

When the young Rhodes returns to England to study for his degree at Oxford, we see him scurry across a snowy quadrangle on his way to Sir John Ruskin's lecture in the Sheldonian Theatre. This brief moment, which establishes that Rhodes is now back in England, was filmed on a warm African afternoon in June at King Edward VII School – Johannesburg's equivalent to Eton or Harrow – using fake snow.

Johannesburg's other exclusive school, St John's College, served as the interior of Cannon Street Hall, where Rhodes informs his triumphant shareholders that they own 'everything in Africa except the air', while Johannesburg's City Hall

The Old Raadsaal, the former seat of government in Pretoria, doubled for the Cape Parliament

doubled as the interior of Windsor Castle – with a great deal of help from the production's art department. The city's exclusive Rand Club, of which Rhodes was a founder member, opened its doors to filming for the first time ever after lengthy negotiations with representatives from the production who were uncharacteristically dressed in formal suits and ties – still required dress in this bastion of white male supremacy. The club was used to represent the London hotel where Rhodes stays with his secretary, Harry Currey, when he rushes to England to urge politicians and businessmen to support his exploits in Africa following Queen Victoria's repudiation of the concession he fraudulently acquired from King Lobengula.

A large number of private and public nineteenth-century buildings in Johannesburg, nearby Pretoria and the surrounding area were used throughout the series. Scenes that take place in the Cape Parliament were filmed in Pretoria's Old Raadsaal, the former seat of government of the Boer republic the Transvaal and latterly of the old South Africa, which now stands empty, a forlorn reminder of its iniquitous past.

One of the biggest problems facing the producers was finding a building to represent the magnificent presidential home, Groote Schuur ('Great Barn'), that Rhodes had built in 1892 beneath Table Mountain at Cape Town.

'Groote Schuur is a beautiful building but the rooms are surprisingly small,' explains Maurice Cain. 'The house was a huge statement of power and wealth by Rhodes but its grandeur and significance wouldn't have come across on screen, so we had to find a suitable alternative, somewhere in our area.'

Once again, the production achieved a 'first', when it obtained permission to film for three weeks at the presidential guest house in Pretoria, within the grounds of Nelson Mandela's official residence, where HM the Queen and Prince Philip stayed during their state visit to South Africa in 1994. 'The guest house is really Groote Schuur on a larger scale, as the two buildings were designed by the same architect,' says Maurice Cain. 'It was the perfect solution to our problem, and as it's an official state building full of priceless relics and antiques we were immensely grateful to the authorities for granting us permission to film there.'

The varied landscape of Nash's Farm served as a backdrop to most of the scenes that take place in open African territory. It was, however, short of one crucial natural feature – a river. There are several key scenes in the series involving rivers. In uncharted territory such as southern Africa in Rhodes's time, rivers were natural territorial borders, so they play a significant part in the story. When the young Rhodes crosses the Orange river at the start of the series, it marks his departure from Cape Colony and his approach to Kimberley. And when Dr Jameson leads his 'pioneer' army across the River Tati in 1890, he is leaving British territory to challenge the might of the Matabele king, Lobengula.

Finding a wide, shallow river in untamed country within easy reach of Johannesburg that would serve for all the river-crossing scenes proved to be one of the most difficult problems of the entire shoot. 'We covered hundreds of miles in the Transvaal in search of a suitable river,' says Cain. 'Finally, we settled on the Vaal river in the Orange Free State, just over 60 miles [around 100 kilometres] north of our base.'

The most difficult river crossing to stage was in episode six when Dr Jameson and Frank Johnson lead a column of soldiers, gun carriages and waggons into Matabeleland, a scene that involved some 80 horses. It had to be shot in its entirety without danger to the actors or the horses, so the stunt and special effects teams were dispatched to the Vaal several weeks beforehand to come up with a safe solution. 'If a horse puts its hoof in a tiny pothole it could break its leg,' explains stunt co-ordinator Gerry Crampton, 'so we had to make the riverbed safe to give the horses a sure footing.' The team worked with the art department for 10 days constructing a submerged platform of sandbags and matting across the entire width of the river for the horses to proceed across safely.

Of course, the submerged road could not be visible to the cameras, which meant it was also invisible to the riders who were guiding the horses. 'We got around that problem by placing strategic clumps of fake reeds and rushes in the water to mark the route,' says Charles Salmon.

To maximize the dramatic effect of each river crossing, the scenes were all shot from several different camera positions. To get from one side of the river to the other by road would have involved a journey of over an hour, as opposed to the few minutes it took by water. A whole team of 'River Rats', members of the local boating club, provided dinghies to transport camera and sound equipment, make-up and wardrobe kits, a vast quantity of film paraphernalia and the entire cast and crew from one side of the river to the other. Except, that is, for one unfortunate young assistant, who was assigned the duty of guarding non-essential equipment left on the riverbank while over 100 of his colleagues tucked into a splendid barbecue lunch in the lush green surroundings on the other side – a welcome change after the heat and dust of weeks on Nash's Farm.

THE DIAMOND DIGGINGS

When the young Rhodes first joined his older brother Herbert at New Rush in 1871, the diamond diggings were on a plateau (kopje) 30 feet above level country, 180 yards wide and 220 yards long, which was divided into 600 claims. Herbert had three claims which he handed over to Cecil when he went north in search of gold (a claim was by regulation 31 feet square and divided into four sections). Ten thousand people worked on the kopje, digging, sorting and sieving. The mules and carts, which went along the narrow and unrailed roads, continually tumbled into the chasms below. The young Rhodes was the first prospector to mechanize his claims.

Overleaf:
Lobengula's kraal,
Gubulawayo,
took three
months to build

Chapter 5

Playing Rhodes

MARTIN SHAW

'Politically and emotionally I see Rhodes as a monster, but I couldn't play him like that,' says Martin Shaw of the character he brings to life on screen. 'I can't comment on him while I'm playing him so I put my own beliefs away. I don't play Rhodes from a political standpoint – my only criteria are truthfulness to the character and sympathy to the script.'

Martin Shaw is one of the UK's leading actors. Born in Birmingham, he has enjoyed a prestigious career spanning more than 30 years. He trained at LAMDA, the London Academy of Music and Dramatic Art, and established a family tradition as his three children, Luke, Joe and Sophie, have followed in his footsteps.

His career was launched in 1967 with a string of major roles in theatre and television. Ten years later came the TV role of tough policeman Ray Doyle in *The Professionals*, the part that made him a household name. More recently he played Chief Constable Alan Cade in ITV's long-running police series, *The Chief*. He has won acclaim for numerous stage roles, including *Are You Lonesome Tonight?* in which he played Elvis Presley, and Oscar Wilde's *The Ideal Husband*, which was revived in London's West End soon after he returned from filming in South Africa. He was subsequently nominated for a Tony Award for his performance in the play when it was staged on Broadway in the summer of 1996.

Shaw readily admits that Rhodes was one of the most challenging roles of his career. 'He was an incredibly complex man. He had all the characteristics of a megalomaniac, but with immense personal charm. It's easy to see him in retrospect as a nineteenth-century Napoleon, Hitler or Saddam Hussein, but he embodied the spirit of the age. It's very dangerous to impose twentieth-century perceptions on nineteenth-century imperialist ideals and it's something I had to avoid doing in order to portray him truthfully.

'My intention with Rhodes was to express his humanity as much as possible, albeit a diseased humanity. He had great emotional intensity yet was unable to

Opposite:

Martin Shaw as

Cecil Rhodes

express his feelings. He always thought he was going to die soon, so he lived his life as a race against time. This was what made the man tick. If I'd just portrayed him as a prototypical fascist it wouldn't have been interesting.'

Another intriguing aspect of Cecil Rhodes's personality was his ambiguous sexuality. He never married and surrounded himself with handsome young men. His deep attachments to two of them in particular, Neville Pickering (played by Ray Coulthard) and Harry Currey (Gresby Nash), had a profound effect on his life. 'The circumstantial evidence of his homosexuality is overwhelming,' says Shaw. 'It was widely known that he didn't like women and that he formed very intense relationships with a certain type of young man. Even Queen Victoria asked him if it was true that he was a woman-hater. There was no understanding or even acknowledgement of the concept of homosexuality at that time. I suspect he was a deeply repressed homosexual but that his homosexuality was never consummated.'

Shaw was first approached about the part in the early stages of development of the project. 'I was enormously excited at the time, but actors are often offered parts in productions that never come to fruition. The biggest surprise was hearing that it was actually going ahead ten years on, in South Africa, where I would never have worked before the political changes.'

The best surprise, however, was hearing that his son, Joe, had won the part of the younger Rhodes. 'I knew that the producers were looking for an actor to play my younger self, so I suggested that they might consider Joe. We don't look that alike but we have a very similar build and there is a definite family resemblance in our body language and mannerisms. Nevertheless Joe was an unknown quantity as an actor, and he had to win the part himself to convince the producers and director that he was up to the job.'

Casting father and son in the same role meant that Martin and Joe were never actually working at the same time, but before filming started they spent time together, sharing their research and discussing the characteristics of the extraordinary man they were both playing.

The disjointed nature of filming, with entirely different scenes from different periods being shot out of order, meant that their schedules occasionally overlapped. Martin was on set for Joe's nerve-racking first day, but kept discreetly in the background. Six weeks later he flew back to South Africa two days early to watch Joe's last day of shooting, by which time his son had emerged as an accomplished and confident young actor.

'It was very gratifying sharing the role with Joe,' he says. 'It sounds corny but I couldn't help remembering him as a tiny baby, and now he's a professional actor starring in one of television's biggest-ever productions. I guess I'm a very proud dad.'

Despite weeks of preparation for the role, Martin Shaw admits, 'On the first day of filming I was absolutely terrified. I knew the script, I'd seen the sets and I'd had numerous costume fittings and make-up tests so I knew exactly how I was going to look at each stage of Rhodes's life. But until I opened my mouth I didn't know how I was going to sound. No matter how much you prepare, you never quite know what's going to happen until you get in front of the camera.'

To make Martin's task even more difficult, his first day of filming involved Rhodes in his middle years. Luckily those around him understood the difficulties this can present for an actor. 'My nerves were eased as soon as I saw my costume. I'd last seen it when it was newly made, but since then Lyn Avery, our costume designer, had aged it beautifully. It looked well worn, with creases round the elbow – this is the sort of thing an actor really appreciates. Then I walked onto the set of Rhodes's study and sat down at his desk to spend a few moments alone. When I opened the drawer I couldn't believe my eyes. Although the viewers will never see inside, Maurice Cain had filled it with replicas of Rhodes's letter paper and period office paraphernalia. The attention to detail and thoughtfulness knocked me out. I rifled around and handled his things and I could feel what it would have been like to be Rhodes. It gave me confidence in the role and in the whole production.'

Although Rhodes's story is the conquest of a continent, he was a great manipulator who wielded his power largely from behind desks in smoke-filled rooms in Kimberley and the Cape Parliament. He left the negotiations and bloody confrontations with the Matabele to his trusted accomplices. Inevitably these aspects of the story didn't actually involve Martin Shaw in filming but, such was his

Martin Shaw arrives on location to share Joe's last day of filming. They share a joke with director David Drury

enthusiasm, he couldn't resist turning up on set as a spectator, video camera in hand, to shoot his own personal record of the production. 'I'm a history freak,' he says. 'I love trying to find out what life was really like for people in other eras. On our sets you felt like a genuine onlooker of nineteenth-century pioneer life. It was all so authentic — it gave me a great buzz just watching. We had horses, battles, hurricanes, thousands of extras. It was like making a Western — a *Boy's Own* dream come true.'

Despite his obvious delight in all aspects of the production, he was considerably less thrilled at having to spend so much time in Johannesburg. 'It's not an organic city. There's no river, no port, no natural reason why a city would have grown up here. It was founded at the end of the last century with the discovery of gold, so it's a city built entirely on greed. It's full of negative energy and I'm convinced that's one of the reasons why it's such a dangerous, violent place.'

The other reason, of course, is its troubled history of racial division and conflict — a history in which Cecil Rhodes played such a crucial part. The irony does not escape Shaw. 'Everything that I dislike about Johannesburg goes back to Rhodes,' he says. 'The lust for gold and diamonds on which the city was founded, and apartheid. Rhodes was the architect of apartheid. It never occurred to him that a country belonged to anyone else — it was just there for the taking. South Africa has paid the price for that attitude, and will long continue to do so.'

An original photograph of Rhodes is recreated by the art department and Martin Shaw

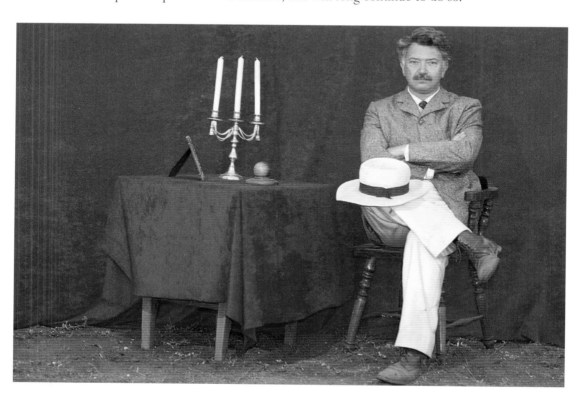

JOE SHAW

'Being Martin Shaw's son got me to the front of the queue, but it didn't get me in the door – I had to do that myself,' says young Joe Shaw of the part that has set him on the road to stardom. The 22-year-old drama student left LAMDA a term early in his final year to take the part of the young Cecil Rhodes. It is his first professional role.

He was on a tour of the Netherlands with his drama school when he heard that David Drury wanted to meet him. 'I'd heard about the production from my dad but I couldn't imagine why the director wanted to see me. It was all chaotic as we were moving around from place to place and I couldn't be contacted easily, but eventually we arranged to meet at Amsterdam airport. I was still in the dark as to why we were meeting, but the next thing I knew I was being flown to London to read for the part. Just a few days later I heard that I'd got it. I couldn't believe it – and neither could my friends. They all said "You lucky bastard!" and then added "well done, you deserve it", which was nice.

'Dad and I worked closely together on the scripts. We had to sort out our approach, because he was playing the man I became, and I was playing the boy he was. We both did our own research and shared what we found, deciding what to go with and what to ignore. I learned that Rhodes was one of a family of nine children and that his father was a very strict parson. His brothers went to Winchester and Eton but Rhodes went to a village school because of his poor health. All his life he was restricted, then he came to Africa and the world was his oyster. He always wanted to be taken seriously and had a seriousness beyond his years. Even in his twenties he liked to be called "Old Man".'

Joe was thrilled to learn that he was going to spend even longer in South Africa than he'd anticipated. His part of the filming was to take six weeks, but his total stay in the country would be twelve. He wasn't quite so thrilled when he found out that this was because he had to learn to ride. 'I've been scared of horses since I was kicked by one when I was young, so the prospect of having to gallop across open country, Western-style, with one hand on the reins and no bit in the horse's mouth was absolutely terrifying.' Once out in South Africa, he was taken to the production unit's stables and introduced to Gavin Mey, the horse master, and Gerry Crampton, the stunt co-ordinator. 'Gavin and Gerry were terrific – they really built up my confidence. By the end of the shoot I was riding at every possible opportunity.'

Joe Shaw plays the young Rhodes

One incident shook his confidence badly, however. When the young Rhodes and his manservant Christmas (played by Patrick Shai) first arrive at New Rush mine, they meet up with Rhodes's eccentric older brother, Herbert. He joins them on their cart and they trot along a rocky track, high above the open diamond diggings below. The camera was lined up for a close-up shot of the horse pulling away, with Herbert at the reins. There were several false starts as 'action!' was called, but the horse seemed reluctant to move. Fearing that neither the horse nor the crew would ever respect him again, Tim Dutton, who plays Herbert, gave one final over-assertive crack of the whip and the horse shot off at a gallop. The crew looked on aghast as the fragile cart careered along the track with a sheer drop below. All three actors were clinging on for their lives as Dutton tried desperately to bring the horse under control.

'I honestly thought it was the end for all of us,' says Joe Shaw. 'Then a miracle happened. A hand stretched between us, grabbed the reins and managed to bring the horse to a halt. It was Gavin Mey, our horse master.'

Unbeknown to the actors, as the horse bolted Gavin had leaped towards the back of the cart and clung on by his fingertips. Hauling himself up James Bond-style, he manoeuvred himself over the trunks on board and seized the reins. 'When you work with horses you have to have quick reactions,' he says modestly. The actors' nerves were badly shaken but reliving the moment over a few stiff drinks that night served to restore their confidence and the next day they were back behind the reins – this time keeping a very close eye on the horse master's whereabouts.

Joe has always been close to his famous father but he admits that the prospect of working together gave him some anxiety. 'It could have been like being taught to drive by a relative – disastrous because you're too close. He's a frighteningly good actor, which is also scary. I felt a tremendous amount of pressure to do a good job. I didn't want people to think that I only got the part because my dad was playing Rhodes.'

In the event, none of these worries proved to be a problem. 'Dad helped me a lot in the initial approach to the part but he didn't intrude at all – in fact he was out of the country when I was doing most of my work.' Towards the end of Joe's stay, Martin returned to South Africa and they spent an evening viewing a rough compilation of all Joe's scenes. 'I thought it would be excruciating because I'd never

Joe Shaw as the young Rhodes

seen myself on screen before. I found it impossible to judge my performance but Dad seemed happy so I decided it couldn't be too bad.'

He was delighted when his father turned up to share his last day on location. Such is the topsy-turvy nature of filming that this was actually Joe's first scene in the series – Rhodes's arrival in southern Africa with his manservant, Christmas. 'It was the best day of the whole shoot,' Joe remembers. 'We had to cross a wide river on a horse-drawn cart. The horses were quite nervous at first so we had to do numerous takes that involved being transported to various parts of the river in rubber dinghies. I was allowed to do all my own driving and it was brilliant.'

For Joe Shaw, playing the young Cecil Rhodes was a dream come true. 'I've always wanted to be an actor – I can't ever remember wanting to do anything else. Making *Rhodes* was a brilliant adventure. My only worry is that I won't ever get a better part, but good parts aren't restricted to big productions. In this case I've had both. Rhodes was such a complex, multi-layered character. It was the most intensive training course I could ever have wished for.'

Joe's favourite day of filming was driving a horse-drawn waggon across the River Vaal with Patrick Shai (Christmas)

Chapter 6

Shooting *Rhodes*

FILMING — WHY DOES IT TAKE SO LONG?

It took six months to shoot all eight episodes of *Rhodes* — 132 days of shooting to bring just under nine hours of television to the screen. For 26 weeks the same crew toiled away, working mostly six-day weeks for at least 12 hours a day, with only one two-week respite from filming. Because of the scale of the production, Ken Stott, who plays Barney Barnato, finished work four months before Frances Barber even started her role as Princess Radziwill.

The series is made of up of 561 scenes, each one consisting of any number of different individual shots or 'set-ups'. A total of 1 543 set-ups was completed, using 374,455 feet of Super 16 mm film. On an average day, the entire production crew of 180 people worked flat out to produce 3.54 minutes of screen time. Fifteen minutes of film was shot for every one minute that ended up on screen. That amounts to barely an hour of actual shooting per day. Why does it take so long? What is everyone doing for the other 11 hours?

The answer is that it's not the filming that takes the time but getting everything ready. It's a bit like lighting the candles on a birthday cake. Before that moment arrives, the recipe will have been chosen, the ingredients bought, prepared and mixed, the utensils used and washed, the oven heated, the cake baked, then iced and decorated. The guests assemble and the candles are finally lit. Then, calamity — the child fails to blow them out, bursts into tears, and you have to re-light the candles and try all over again. Getting to the point where the candles are finally lit is what takes the time in filming. And after all that careful preparation, anything can go wrong at the crucial moment...

Blocking the scene

The director's first assistant and chief technicians will already be familiar with the location or set and should know how the director plans to shoot each scene, but the actors may well be there for the first time. The director starts by 'blocking' the

Opposite:
Martin Shaw
and the camera
crew prepare for
a take

" RHODES "

PROD.				
ROLL	SC	SLATE		TAKE
88	205	222		2
DIRECTOR		DAVID DRURY		
CAMERA		ALEC CURTIS		
DATE		DAY	NIGHT	INT	EXT
13/6/95		FILTER 45R		
		SOUND 75		SYNC

scene with the actors. This is not a full rehearsal but a run-through of the action, working out movements and where the cameras and sound-recording equipment will be in relation to the actors.

The actors then disappear to wardrobe and make-up to be transformed into the character they are playing. For some, preparation will take longer than others: Martin Shaw's make-up for Cecil Rhodes took approximately an hour. Then, they have to wait – sometimes for hours – until they are needed.

Technical preparations

It is the art department's job to ensure that the set is fully dressed, which may entail last-minute adjustments to furniture, furnishings and props, lighting fires, setting clocks, filling glasses, etc. Interior scenes often require elaborate artificial lighting, which takes a long time to set up and adjust precisely to the lighting cameraman's instructions. The gaffer – the chief electrician – works with his assistant (his 'best boy') and a team of electricians – known as 'sparks' – setting up lamps, fine-tuning the lighting and making sure that all cables are safe and out of shot. The construction department may well have to black out windows for night shots or build towers quickly for high camera angles. Interior sets are often extremely cramped, so the camera operator has to work out his positions very carefully to

*The crew of
Rhodes at work in
the kraal*

ensure that the direction is physically possible. If the director wants a moving shot rather than a static one, a track has to be laid by the 'grips' so that the camera can move smoothly (the slightest uneven movement will register and make the whole shot unusable). Measurements are taken to help the focus puller select the right lenses and keep the camera correctly focused throughout the shot, and the camera is checked and loaded. The technicians set up and rehearse their movements using stand-ins – people who literally stand in for the leading actors, who need to conserve their energy for the actual 'take'.

The take

When the set and the technicians are ready, the actors are called from the base, which on *Rhodes* was usually a circle of caravans, often some distance from the film set. The actors arrive fully dressed and made up, accompanied by members of the wardrobe and make-up departments. The scene is then rehearsed with the actors, the camera crew and the 'boom' operator, who records the sound with a microphone on the end of a long extendible pole, which must be kept as close as possible to the actors without ever appearing in shot or casting a shadow. In a scene with a lot of action, this requires a great deal of precision and skill.

At this point, the director or the actors might find that changes need to be made – for example, that it's impossible to get from A to B in one movement, or that it

Moving camera positions on location can take time ...

seems more natural to deliver a line standing up rather than sitting down – in which case lights and cameras have to be moved again. It is only when the director, the actors, the lighting cameraman, the camera operator, the sound recordist and the boom operator are all happy, that the words, 'We'll go for a take' are heard.

It is the signal for a flurry of activity as final checks are made by the wardrobe and make-up departments. Cameras turn over, sound tapes roll, the clapperboard marks the start of the shot so that pictures and sound will be synchronized and complete silence falls. Then, and only then, does the director shout 'action!' If an actor fluffs a line, if a plane passes overhead, if someone inadvertently wanders into shot or makes a noise or if anything at all goes wrong, the director shouts 'cut!' and the whole process starts all over again.

The same set-up is usually shot several times. An actor's performance will vary slightly (or sometimes drastically) in each take. Sometimes several takes are required for an actor to deliver the performance the director is seeking. Often, the director needs several perfectly good takes from which to choose in order to balance or match the rest of the scene when all the shots are cut together. A number of takes may also be required because a scene is technically difficult and keeps going wrong, particularly when tricky camera movements or unpredictable factors such as horses are involved.

This is why even a short scene between two characters in a room can take hours to shoot. During the course of the scene, the viewer may see both characters from several different angles, together and individually. Each different angle is shot separately, with the whole scene being replayed time and time again.

This is the basic process involved in shooting a straightforward scene. Imagine the complications involved in a scene with hundreds of extras and horses, action and dialogue. A very big scene, such as a battle or a river crossing, takes hours to set up, so it's impossible to replay the whole scene over and over again for one camera in different positions. To capture such scenes in *Rhodes*, three or four cameras were used in different positions to cut down on the number of takes required. It took longer to set these scenes up, but they were covered from more angles, more quickly.

DOWN ON NASH'S FARM

Hazards

Most of the filming took place on the somewhat inappropriately named Nash's Farm, actually a vast area of private land about the size of Hampshire, 20 miles (32 kilometres) north of Johannesburg. Although only a 40-minute drive from the city, it is completely uninhabited and inhospitable open country. Part of the farm is a private game reserve where giraffe, gazelle, impala and zebra roam freely. No-one quite believed the rumour that leopard also live there, until several animal carcasses were found and the Zulus working on Lobengula's kraal confirmed that the tracks nearby did indeed match those of a leopard.

One crew member had an encounter with the local wildlife that was rather too close for comfort. In the early stages of the building of Kimberley, the construction team continued working until after dark one night, when they were stopped by a violent thunderstorm. The workers left the site, leaving the construction manager to make everything secure. When he went to leave, his truck engine had flooded and wouldn't start. All he could do was sit and wait, in the hope that someone would realize he hadn't returned to base. As the minutes passed, he could hear hyenas drawing ever closer, until eventually they were circling the truck. Fortunately, his absence was noticed and a rescue party sent out.

Nash's Farm is an ideal habitat for poisonous snakes, including the puff adder – larger and more venomous than Britain's native species – and the lethal cobra. When props and equipment were stored in an old shack near Lobengula's kraal, no-one realized that they had invaded the home of a cobra. One day an unwary electrician entered and the cobra reared up and spat its potentially deadly venom at him, which required two days of treatment. Because Nash's Farm is a protected game reserve, no animals or snakes could be killed so the onus was on the crew to be vigilant at all times. They were advised to make plenty of noise and vibration while working and to stamp and thrash around, particularly on new territory.

The same caution was required for poisonous spiders, which lurk in dark corners and only bite if disturbed. A wolf spider, a particularly large and dangerous creature, found itself a cosy corner on the electricians' truck, which was evacuated rather hastily by a group of burly men who weren't too keen on their new travelling companion.

Tick-bite fever is also a serious hazard in the summer months, as it causes inflammation of the brain and spinal column. Both Charles Salmon and Maurice Cain fell victim to it and suffered extreme 'flu-like symptoms for two weeks. 'You're not aware when a tick bites you, but it attaches itself to your flesh and burrows in,' explains Salmon. 'We had a big notice at the production base saying 'Check yourself for ticks!' We weren't taking any chances, even in the winter. I suppose we were once bitten, twice shy!'

Transport and communication

In such remote territory, communication and safety were top priorities. Mobile phones didn't always work, so the production set up radio stations at the horse department's stables on the edge of Nash's Farm, as well as at the production base at Zenex.

The roads on Nash's Farm are nothing more than dirt tracks scattered with rocks and large boulders and were often quite steep. 'Because of the bad driving conditions we had to have unit and transport managers to service the needs of a large crew in such remote locations,' explains Salmon. 'They had to maintain the roads, which needed frequent levelling, and all the vehicles, and had to monitor all

The film unit really did look like a travelling circus

comings and goings to make sure that no-one went missing. In theory, they knew the exact whereabouts of every member of the cast and crew at any time.'

Driving on dirt tracks requires extreme caution, but despite severe warnings the first accident occurred only days into the production. A car that was being driven far too fast shot off the road and turned over. Fortunately, no-one was injured, but the car was a write-off. 'We decided to leave the wrecked car where it had ended up, in full view of the road. We thought it would serve as a reminder of the dangers and it seemed to work.'

The huge distances involved in getting anywhere in South Africa means that a car is essential, although the largely underprivileged black population still has to rely on public transport. Because the black cast and crew had to travel at the crack of dawn and late at night from the townships of Alexandria and Soweto on the furthest outskirts of Johannesburg, the production laid on its own bus services.

Servicing the unit

The logistics of producing a series on this scale in such remote territory are enormously complex. The number of shooting crew involved in filming each day was about a hundred, plus actors and extras, or 'crowd'. On an average day, around 150 people would be on set, all needing transport, toilets, food and water – and, for the actors, costumes and make-up. Bigger days, of which there were many, required a crowd of 400 as well as additional crew, so total numbers of 600 were quite common.

Even the most basic amenities had to be planned for. There is no water on Nash's Farm, so the production laid on its own supplies by digging pools and lining them with plastic to make mini-reservoirs and using agricultural containers to fill water bowsers.

Just like an army, a film crew marches on its stomach. Filming is a physically exhausting business, especially in a difficult and unfamiliar environment. As well as main meals – breakfast and lunch, and supper if filming was going on late – the crew needed a continual supply of drinks to avoid dehydration and snacks to keep them going.

Local caterers were hired who were used to the complications of servicing film productions. Because of concerns about hygiene, the food was cooked every day at a nearby base, sealed and taken to the location where hot-plates were used to keep it warm. The same food was available for all, including massive supplies of 'pap' or mealie meal (boiled finely ground maize) which is the staple diet of black South Africans.

The caterers regularly had to feed over 600 people in an hour. It was the job of the third assistant directors to keep an eye on the food queue and make sure that anyone not needed immediately on set either had their food before the main rush, or held back. 'We couldn't risk key crew members or leading actors being stuck at the back of the queue,' says Charles Salmon. At least with large numbers of Zulu extras around, waiting in line was never dull – singing queues were a regular feature of life on set.

Nash's Farm looks magnificent, but it is not the ideal surroundings for alfresco eating. In the winter, the altitude of 6000 feet meant high winds that whipped up the natural dust, as well as the additional dust laid for the production, while towards the end of the shoot as summer approached the heat was relentless. Catering tents were essential to serve the food and to provide shelter for those eating it – often a mixture of Victorian ladies and gentlemen, diamond diggers, 'pioneer' soldiers, scantily clad warriors and twentieth-century film crew.

Drinks and snacks were the domain of Rosie, who was never once seen without her large, red, broad-brimmed hat, on top of which she would balance large containers of water or squash. Her apron was emblazoned with the words 'Rosie – Crew Mama' and she took her responsibilities very seriously. As the crew was constantly on the move, so was Rosie. Her determination to have her table of drinks in the right place at the right time meant that she just kept moving, whether or not the camera was pointing in her direction. 'If viewers catch a glimpse of a large red hat in the middle of a Zulu battle, that will be Rosie,' says Neil Pearson, who plays Dr Jameson.

On the move

There were several major permanent sets built on Nash's Farm around which would gather 'the unit' – camera and lighting trucks, wardrobe and make-up buses, caravans for the artists, catering tents, trucks for the livestock and the ubiquitous mobile toilets. However, large parts of the story take place in the open veld, so then the unit would be on the move.

This travelling circus would trundle miles from the security of the production base across rough, featureless country. If anything crucial – a prop, an item of costume, some technical equipment or indeed a person – was left behind, it could hold up filming for a couple of hours. If a vehicle broke down, or got stuck on a steep part of the track, the whole convoy would be delayed. As mobile phones often didn't work in such remote places there might be no contact with the production office all day.

Even finding the unit could be a problem. Maps were little help as Nash's Farm has no roads, and with nothing but grassland and rolling hills as far as the eye could see the only indication of the unit's location at any given time was a cloud of dust from a moving vehicle.

Burning Lobengula's kraal

One of the most exciting days of filming of the entire shoot was the burning of Lobengula's kraal, which features in the opening titles. In episode six of the series, when the old king finally senses defeat, he orders his kraal to be torched and abandons it to Rhodes's conquering 'pioneer' army. After months of dedicated work building Gubulawayo and several weeks spent filming there, the day came when the magnificent set of Zulu huts was to be burned to the ground. The kraal was made entirely from wood and grass. Once it caught fire it would be obliterated in minutes. There could be no false starts, no second chances and no accidents. The set had almost been devastated by a massive bushfire only weeks before (see Chapter 8), and now the unit that had fought those flames had to stage a fire on a huge scale in the parched veld without endangering any people, animals or equipment.

The scene required a procession of women and children to exit from the kraal in ox-drawn waggons, while the bulky Lobengula is hoisted on a throne onto the shoulders of his *indunas*. As they make a dignified exit, his warriors run amok with blazing torches, igniting the grass huts. By the time the king's procession reaches the massive stockade gates, the entire kraal is an inferno.

Lobengula's procession makes a hasty exit as the kraal is torched

As the fire could only be staged once, four fixed cameras were to cover the action from all angles, while a 'steadicam' – a mobile camera literally strapped to its operator – would be right in the thick of things, able to turn 360 degrees. Naturally one camera couldn't be within sight of another, including the steadicam, so the whole scene had to be blocked out and planned in immense detail. On screen it looks like a frenzy of chaos and confusion but in reality every movement was meticulously planned and rehearsed.

The actors carrying out the torching were Zulu extras who didn't speak a word of English, so the Zulu co-ordinator, Bobby Duffas, had to relay every direction and safety warning to them in their own language.

The kraal was an inferno in seconds

While the actors were rehearsing the scene and the camera operators refining their positions, the special effects team and the fire brigade prepared for the inferno and the immediate aftermath. There were three priorities: capturing the full drama of the fire on camera, ensuring that it could be contained afterwards and, most important of all, the safety of everyone on set. First assistant John Watson gathered the camera crews together and gave them a grave warning: 'No heroics. If you're in danger, run, just get away. Don't stay to protect your equipment, or to help anyone else. You'll be putting yourself in danger as well.'

No-one who had experienced the earlier bushfire needed reminding of the speed and ferocity of the flames. By now a huge crowd of onlookers had gathered – actors not involved in the scene, crew who would not normally be on set – anyone remotely connected with the production wanted to share the excitement. This created a problem for the assistant directors. Because the steadicam would be pointing in all directions, there was only one small area where spectators would be out of shot. The crowd jostled to get as close as possible to the action, but as the tension mounted and the dangers were spelled out, they jostled to get further away.

Once again, Bobby Duffas gathered his team of Zulu extras and relayed their final instructions to them. They took up their positions, this time with torches blazing. There was a deathly hush – far more intense than the usual silence – as John Watson confirmed that the safety officers had made their final checks and that each camera crew was ready with cameras turning. The word that hadn't been heard for five hours – 'action!' – echoed across Nash's Farm. On the distant horizon a giraffe glided gracefully towards a tree. The procession of oxen, women and children made its way steadily towards the stockade gates and the mighty Washington Sixolo, who plays Lobengula, was hoisted high above the shoulders of his fellow actors. Warriors ran among them, darting from hut to hut and igniting each one.

The kraal was an instant fireball, its flames roaring in the high wind and seeming to touch the sky. In the midst of the inferno, Lobengula and his men lumbered towards the gates chanting their mournful acknowledgement of defeat.

Discipline almost broke down, fear taking over, as the fire reached terrifying proportions within seconds. 'Run, run, run!' could be heard above the roar of the scorching flames. No-one stayed to shout 'cut!' The camera technicians hovered, then bolted, leaving their cameras turning. Spectators scattered in all directions, stumbling over rocks and logs as they felt the heat of the fire on their backs.

As the fire brigade moved in and took control, the crew, actors and onlookers flocked back, dragging equipment clear and looking for their friends in the dense smoke. The flames died down, the smoke cleared – and then one spark flew out into the veld, instantly setting it alight. For one long minute the prospect of another bushfire loomed, but this time it was quickly doused and contained.

Everyone was safe, the equipment undamaged and the inferno had been captured on film. And Lobengula's kraal, the lovingly created stronghold of Gubulawayo, lay in smouldering ruins. Exactly as planned.

Washington Sixolo plays Lobengula, King of the Matabele, who stood between Rhodes and his dream of extending the British Empire from the Cape to Cairo

The man who made *Rhodes*

'How would you like to direct *Stagecoach* meets *Citizen Kane* meets *Indiana Jones?*' This was the question that Scott Meek asked director David Drury over a drink in 1994. 'I started to tell him about the series, and after three minutes I knew he was hooked!'

From that moment Drury was committed to directing the BBC's most ambitious drama production ever. It's unusual for one director to work on an entire series of this length – it's an exhausting process, from which there is no respite. The director has the ultimate creative responsibility for everything that you see and hear on screen and, from the moment the cast and crew assemble on set, he is in charge. Preparation is everything. Together with his camera team, headed by director of photography Alec Curtis and his first assistant John Watson, David Drury carried out detailed recces of every location and set before shooting started, working out and discussing how he intended to shoot each scene, where he would put the cameras and how the action would be played out.

Once shooting begins the director is on set for every minute of the working day. Scenes are not shot in chronological order so the director must have a clear sense of continuity and pace – which scene will eventually follow which and the mood and energy required for them to flow seamlessly – without ever losing sight of the narrative thrust.

Directing a series the length and scale of *Rhodes* was the ultimate challenge, which required enormous mental and physical stamina. 'It's like directing three John Ford movies, back-to-back,' says Drury. 'Outside of the cinema you rarely see action on this scale, and even in the cinema it's unusual these days, so very few people get the chance to work on something like this. Although it's a period piece the story has tremendous pace and energy. But despite thousands of extras, battles, fires and spectacle, in the final analysis we're telling a story and everything else has to serve that.'

Martin Shaw describes David Drury as the 'ultimate actor's director'. Over and above his 180-strong crew and equipment worth hundreds of thousands of pounds, Drury's principal tools are his actors. Unlike many directors, who block out a scene and fit the actors around the cameras, he works with the actors first and fits the cameras around them.

Director David Drury gets involved in the action

This means that in the big action scenes, such as the burning of Lobengula's kraal, the actors have a 360-degree space in which to work. 'I'm not interested so much in where I can put a fire in relation to the camera, I'm interested in the emotion of the scene, in what the actors are doing. It sounds romantic but emotions are the pulse of any film, not the special effects or fancy camerawork.'

This approach was particularly appreciated by the South African actors, who were largely unused to being consulted by directors and to making a contribution to the creative process. South African actor David Butler, who plays Rudd, the young Rhodes's first partner on the diamond diggings, says: 'David gives actors a lot of time and space to work things through and to offer suggestions. It's a very creative process, and it's not always the rule in this country.'

Washington Sixolo, who plays Lobengula, confirmed this view: 'Working on the series gave every actor, black and white, a new way of working. Local directors, usually white because black directors have not been long in the game, give more instructions. But with David Drury we discussed thoroughly with him what to do. I appreciated that very much.'

'It's true that the South African actors were taken aback when I asked them for their input,' agrees Drury. 'They're not used to this style of direction but they responded magnificently. Until very recently, whites as well as blacks have been living under a repressive regime and it stifled creativity all round. Now it has a chance to flourish and it's great to see.'

He particularly enjoyed working with the black actors and extras. 'It's been a revelation. They're so naturally expressive. After all the years of repression so much energy and passion is being unleashed. They don't have any fear of expressing their inner selves – none of the inhibitions of the white man. We've been learning from them all the time.'

Although the series takes place at the end of the last century, David sees it very much as a story with modern relevance. 'Rhodes was a man before his time. He understood PR – manipulation of the media, the value of intelligence and communication, the control of information. He's a very compelling character because he's so dislikeable. He's like J.R. Ewing – truly Machiavellian. Martin is playing him with great charm, but it's an ironic charm because underneath all that there is something very manipulative and dark, even amoral. I'd like to think that the series is a remarkable journey which is full of mixed signals for the audience. Sometimes we like him, sometimes we don't. At the end I hope we are still left with that as I believe that ambivalence is the mark of sophisticated drama.

'I read no biographies and deliberately did no research so that I had no references other than my own imagination and Antony's scripts. I stick to the parameters of the text – that's the best way I can serve the story. Other people are hired to pay attention to period detail. I'm a dramatist, not a historian, and that was how I approached the project.'

Chapter 7

Costume, Hair and Make-Up

THE WARDROBE KINGDOM

The wardrobe department on *Rhodes* was headed by costume designer Lyn Avery. She and her team of eight were responsible for designing, making or buying the costumes; dressing every actor and extra; attending to the costume requirements and changes in each scene, and maintaining, repairing and laundering the costumes throughout the entire shoot. On a series of the scale of *Rhodes*, it was an awesome task.

The wardrobe department was based at Zenex, the disused petrol station and shopping mall that formed the headquarters of the production. There Lyn Avery set up her kingdom – a workshop, fitting rooms and a vast store crammed with costume rails. As well as the leading actors' costumes there were hundreds of general period costumes for every category of extra: diamond-diggers and prospectors; Boer men, women and children; Victorian ladies and gentlemen; British and Cape politicians; Rhodes's 'pioneer' soldiers, and scores of Matabele natives and warriors. Lyn was most proud of her boot room, a whole room of shelves stacked with over 500 pairs of leather boots and shoes in every size. 'The black Africans had never seen anything like it. They walk huge distances so shoes are a valued commodity. They used to come just to look in amazement.'

Most of the costumes were hired or made in England. The leading actors had costume fittings in advance wherever possible, but mostly Lyn Avery had to estimate the numbers and types of costumes required according to the scripts, adapting and altering them on the spot and making additional costumes as necessary. She recruited a small team of Zulu workers from the townships. They

Above: Lyn Avery with an elaborate Matabele head-dress, made for the production

Opposite: Vusi Kenene plays Lobengula's crown prince

were skilled seamstresses but knew nothing about making period costumes. 'They were so enthusiastic and keen to learn. I had to teach them the importance of handling and organizing the costumes carefully. I took pattern books out from England and taught them to cut period costumes. I left all my reference books there for them in the hope that they would be well-equipped to work on other period dramas. I don't feel that you could possibly work in South Africa at a time of such change and not contribute something to that process.'

Lyn's team spoke a variety of languages between them, including English, Afrikaans, Zulu and Xhosa. However, language was not the only problem in communication. 'We didn't share any points of reference because they've been cut off for so long. I might refer to a film which would have been seen and known all over the world, and they wouldn't have even heard of it. But they were hungry to learn and would always say 'Tell us, tell us about it'. They felt that working on *Rhodes* was putting them in touch with their cultural heritage and history. I found the whole experience profoundly moving.'

Extras dressed as diamond diggers and prospectors

The look

The costumes had to be appropriate for the period, but equally important to Lyn Avery was ensuring that the clothes worn in the African scenes reflected the landscape – the yellows and browns of the African veld, and its essential red dust. 'Although the facilities at Zenex were somewhat primitive, I was spoilt with a massive working area, and with all the space and light I could ever wish for. Our only water supply was a standpipe but we could do everything on the spot. I wanted the costumes to look as if they'd come from the earth but with the sudden, unexpected flashes of colour you find in Africa. We could dye costumes in a tin bath, hang them to dry in the sun and pick up handfuls of red dust to distress them.'

'Breaking down' costumes to make them look old and well-worn is an important element in any period drama that is to look convincing on screen. 'When the diggers' costumes arrived from England they looked far too new for clothes that would have been worn day in and day out on the open diamond diggings. We heard that the art department was testing the wind machines, which would be used to create a hurricane, so we loaded the costumes into a truck and took them to the Kimberley set, where we exposed them to the full onslaught of the duststorm. They would never have looked as good if we had had to do that artificially.'

One of the head-dresses worn by Lobengula's royal guard

Extras

It was important to Lyn Avery that all those participating in the series, from the leading actors to the hundreds of extras, felt happy in their costumes. 'Working on *Rhodes* was so unusual because all our extras were really playing themselves, rather than just being dressed up. Our Zulu extras were simple, uneducated men from villages in Zululand and the hostels of Johannesburg, and they were delighted to wear their traditional costumes. Similarly, our Boer extras were real Boers – big, burly Afrikaners, many of whom still wear traditional full beards. When we were filming a scene at the home of Paul Kruger, the Boer leader, one of the Boer women came to me at the end of a long day and said, 'Today I was my grandmother, I understand now how she felt.'

Some of the extras grew rather too attached to their costumes. The grooms and stable boys in the horse department took part in almost every scene involving horses, so they had the same costumes, which they wore all the time. Because it enhanced the overall effect if costumes were well-worn, Lyn Avery allowed the boys to hold onto their costumes rather than returning them at the end of each day's filming. She eventually discovered that they were living and even sleeping in their costumes as they were considerably warmer and of a better quality than their own clothes.

Dressing Rhodes

As the leading character, Cecil Rhodes's costumes were vitally important. 'Fortunately, there is good verbal and pictorial documentation of Rhodes's style of dress, which was somewhat idiosyncratic,' says Lyn. 'He wore what he felt comfortable in, which is a normal attitude to us but was considered eccentric in his day. He was well known for sporting Oxford tweeds, which he even wore when he first took his seat in the Cape Parliament.'

Having researched the subject closely, Lyn Avery worked closely with Martin Shaw, discussing the psychology of the man and how that would have been reflected in his dress. 'My research told me that Rhodes always wore his clothes tightly buttoned up to his neck. This seemed appropriate for a man with a serious heart condition that was threatening to kill him all his life. It was as if something was about to explode. It also seemed to represent all the emotional repression he harboured within,' she explains.

It is perfectly true that the young Rhodes arrived in Africa wearing his Bishop's Stortford school blazer and cricket flannels, which he kept lovingly and wore – most inappropriately – at the funeral of his close friend, Neville Pickering. Lyn Avery found an original blazer in the Rhodes Museum in Bishop's Stortford and was able to make five exact copies (for continuity purposes) with specially woven material. 'I was delighted to find that his blazer was such a bold pink-and-black stripe. It looks so striking against the African landscape when he first arrives.'

One of Rhodes's most distinctive physical qualities was the extent to which he aged prematurely from a slender young man to becoming stout and bloated by his 40s. 'Martin Shaw is very fit and trim, so we had to find a way of making him look more and more bloated with advancing years. Using padding presents all sorts of problems – it is hot and uncomfortable and tends to be unyielding when the actor moves or sits down, so it can look very obvious.' Nevertheless, cotton Lycra padding specially made in London was the only solution and Martin Shaw had to suffer being swaddled in layers of it around his legs and torso for much of the production – all in the sweltering heat – which he described as 'like wearing several duvets'.

Above:
Martin Shaw as
Cecil Rhodes

The princess

'From my point of view, Frances Barber was brilliant casting,' says Lyn Avery. 'She's a disciplined actress and she understands the demands of period drama. She carries herself regally, and it was possible to give her the shape of a woman with the class and breeding of a Russian princess. She has the perfect hourglass shape for the period – we literally sculpted the clothes on her.'

All the princess's costumes were designed and made from scratch in London, based on Lyn Avery's reading and research. 'She was quite extraordinary and very eccentric and I wanted her clothes to reflect that.' Even her jewellery, the Radziwill family diamonds and emeralds, was faithfully copied for the production.

Opposite:
Frances Barber as
Princess Catherine
Radziwill

Lyn Avery decided that the princess would undoubtedly have dressed in Paris with clothes by Worth, and was lucky enough to be given the black silk train from an original Worth evening dress from which she made the dress worn by the princess when she first meets Rhodes in England. 'We wanted the Scarlett O'Hara effect – a simple but stunning dress that would undercut all the other women at the event.

'Research gives you your foundation – then you depart from it. When I arrived on my first recce to South Africa I saw brilliant, vivid flowers everywhere. I hoped and prayed that my leading actress would be able to wear these colours, and Frances could. I designed a lilac dress for her to wear when she first visits Rhodes at Groote Schuur because we were using Nelson Mandela's presidential guest house in Pretoria for those scenes and I knew we would be shooting in October when the jacaranda trees are in full purple blossom.'

It is well documented that Princess Radziwill chose to wear a shocking pink dress to court when she was charged with forging Rhodes's signature on cheques and promissory notes. 'When I first saw the brilliant pinks and reds of the protea, Africa's national flower, which grows wild, I knew that this would be the colour of the dress she wears in court, defying contemporary formality and convention.'

Matabele costumes

Lyn Avery's brief before shooting started was to supply 500 costumes for the Matabele natives and warriors, including Lobengula, his royal guard and his *indunas* or councillors. 'I researched and designed the Matabele costumes very carefully, working closely with our Zulu advisor, Barry Leitch. The Matabele was a warrior nation and in old photographs and pictures they look very frightening. Their tribal dress was all taken from nature and they blended in perfectly with the landscape. I saw an aloe tree on the horizon during an early recce and I realized that in 1870, in uncharted territory, I wouldn't have known if it was a tree, an animal, or a Matabele warrior.'

She had hoped that costumes and props would be available from other films about the Zulus made in South Africa, but they had all perished. Everything had to be made from scratch, using fake skins for protected species, as well as cow and goat hides and ostrich feathers, which were bought by the kilo for the elaborate headdresses of the warrior chiefs and royal guard.

One memory she will always treasure is the day a coachload of Zulu extras was brought from their hostel in Johannesburg for a mass costume fitting. They stood in a long line outside the wardrobe department at Zenex, not really understanding why they were there. 'When they stripped off and put on their costumes, they *loved* them. They were so delighted that they broke into spontaneous singing and danced their way between my long line of shirts drying on the washing lines. I'll never forget their pure joy.'

On the days of shooting big scenes at Lobengula's kraal, or the battle scenes, Lyn and her team were up before dawn, dressing over 400 extras before the arrival of the main unit and leading actors.

'Wardrobe departments have a tried-and-tested formula for dealing with large crowds. The extras queued up outside the wardrobe marquee and were given their costumes and a large orange bag for their own clothes, which they hung on a peg. They emerged from the other side of the tent fully dressed and inspected.'

There was only one aspect of the costume which presented a problem to the Zulus, and that was their underpants. Lyn Avery's team made hundreds of little jersey jockstraps that would be invisible under the costumes, which were collected and washed at the end of each day, ready to be worn again. The Zulus balked at first but put them on as instructed. She then realized, to her horror, that they were sneaking their own underpants back on and slipping their packets of cigarettes inside. 'We had to have regular underpants checks, but despite all our efforts I live in dread of spotting a pair of brightly coloured twentieth-century Y-fronts in the middle of a battle scene.'

Another problem was footwear for the Matabele, who traditionally went barefoot. That wasn't possible for the extras on the stony, thorny ground of Nash's Farm, so 'invisible' footwear had to be found. After various experiments and budget considerations, Lyn kitted her front-liners out with black rubber-soled sandals and the rest of the crowd with cheap trainers, dyed to match their skin.

Five hundred Matabele costumes were made for the production

'Pioneer' army uniforms

Rhodes personally designed the uniform worn by the soldiers in his 'pioneer' army. Lyn Avery admits that she was horrified when she first saw photographs of the real thing as, to her eyes, their brown corduroy jackets, riding breeches and boots looked camp and comical. Nevertheless, the uniforms are so well documented that she felt she had to stick to the facts and reproduce them faithfully, so she ordered 120 uniforms to be made up by a military tailor in England. 'They had to be sturdy enough to withstand being worn over and over again for riding, crossing rivers and for going into battle. I was still unsure about the overall look, until I saw them being worn against the backdrop of Africa. Suddenly they looked right and I realized that Rhodes hadn't been such a bad designer after all.'

The 'pioneer' army assembles at Kimberley

HAIR AND MAKE-UP

RoseAnn Samuel, chief hair and make-up artist on *Rhodes*, had her own particular bugbears. 'Because the series covers a period of 30 years and we were shooting everything out of sequence, our biggest concern was continuity.' She had only a short time in pre-production to see the actors and to work out exactly how each character should look at each stage of the story, allowing for natural ageing and circumstances in the script — whether characters were ill or wounded, or had spent long periods in the bush, for example. To remind her of the appearance of each character in every scene, copious notes and Polaroid photographs were taken. 'It was like working on several feature films rolled into one,' she says. 'There were only three of us – myself and my assistants Gill Rees and Elaine Nicholas Browne – and we had to make up nearly 200 characters throughout the series, and more often than not we also had at least 150 extras on set. We had to make up diamond diggers who spent their lives in the dust and filth of the open mines, cleanly coiffed Victorian men and women, mustachioed politicians and statesmen, bearded Boers, rough-and-ready soldiers and hundreds of Matabele warriors.'

The make-up bus

Unlike the production designer or the costume designer, who had permanent bases for their departments, RoseAnn's 'kingdom' was mobile. The make-up bus travels with the unit and is equipped with washbasins, lights, mirrors and all the equipment and kit the team needs to transform the huge cast. Early on in the shoot the make-up bus suffered an accident while it was being moved from one location to another overnight and got stuck on a rock. 'Unfortunately, the driver and his helper panicked,' RoseAnn Samuel says. 'They started to unload the bus, and then didn't know what to do so they dumped everything and abandoned it – including all our make-up kits, notes and photographs. We managed to retrieve most of it the next day, but it was a terrible moment. I begged the driver to leave everything intact if a similar situation arose – which it did – but the same thing happened again. It was just part and parcel of filming in an environment with language and communication problems.'

For the next month while the bus was being repaired, the make-up team had to work in a touring caravan with no running water, which meant the actors had to wash their hair under a camp shower. 'Luckily we were all in the same boat and everyone approached the production with a spirit of adventure. It was the only way to get through.'

Making up Rhodes

In working on the make-up for Cecil Rhodes, RoseAnn Samuel had two main problems to overcome. One was that the same character was being played by two different people – Martin Shaw and his son Joe. The other was that Rhodes, over a period of 30 years, aged very dramatically. Although he was only 48 when he died, because of his heart condition – and possibly his drinking habits – he looked like a man in his 70s, with white hair, a bloated, ruddy face and bulging eyes.

'I started by researching photographs of Rhodes, but they are mostly of him in the later part of his life, so I had to work backwards from there. I met Martin and Joe for a make-up session so that I could experiment with them. I had to work out to what extent Joe could be aged, and how far Martin could be made to look younger. Facially they are not alike, but they have a family resemblance, which helped.'

She decided that she couldn't do a great deal to age Joe, other than providing him with a false moustache when he returns to Kimberley from Oxford. 'Joe has such a baby face and smooth, taut, young skin,' she sighs. 'It's just not possible to make skin like that look old convincingly without using prosthetics, and I knew we wouldn't have time on set for such a long, complicated process – especially as we were shooting out of sequence.'

Martin's ageing process was more complex. 'On any given day, we would be shooting scenes that required Martin to be at his youngest, at his oldest, and in his middle years. To save time, I had to simplify the process. With practice, I could make up Martin as Rhodes at his oldest in just under an hour...Hopefully viewers will suppose that we shot the entire series in sequence, from 1871 to 1902,' she says.

Even at his oldest, Rhodes had a full head of hair. 'Luckily both Martin and Joe have thick hair. They grew it for the production and I permed it. I would then tong their hair before every scene, and for scenes with Martin looking older, I added in grey hairpieces. Martin grew his own moustache that I would lighten or darken as necessary.'

RoseAnn Samuel checks Martin Shaw's make-up before a take

As Rhodes aged, his eyes became bulbous and bleary. 'Martin has very clear, healthy, piercing blue eyes,' RoseAnn Samuel stresses. 'This was fine for Rhodes's younger years, but they weren't right for an ageing, ailing man. We solved that problem by having special contact lenses made with white rims that have the effect of clouding his eyes.'

Martin's florid, bloated face as Rhodes grew older was due to a combination of her skill and Martin's acting expertise. 'I gave him broken veins and puffy eyes by using make-up. If I'd had more time each day I might have chosen a more elaborate process of using prosthetics and literally adding false pieces to his face. But this can often get in the way of the actor's performance. At the end of the day he has to convince the viewers that he's an old man and make-up alone can never do that.'

Wigs, beards and missing moustaches

RoseAnn Samuel was not only responsible for make-up and hairstyling but also for supplying all of the hairpieces – wigs, beards, moustaches and sideburns. These had to be ordered and brought from England as the South African wig-makers didn't meet her stringent quality test. The leading British actors had fittings for moustaches, beards and wigs before they flew out for filming but she had to make head and chin templates of the South African actors and send them back to England to be made.

She also had to take literally thousands of general facial hairpieces for all the extras. 'Keeping track of all the hairpieces was our biggest nightmare. Each moustache was worth about £60 and with the quantity that we needed, the total value was enormous. Every day, huge numbers of hairpieces went missing — people would forget where they put them, stuff them in their pockets, take them off at lunchtime, take them home by mistake, or just generally lose them. We became obsessed with retrieving moustaches, beards and sideburns, which then had to be cleaned and dressed for the next day's filming. I even started dreaming about them.'

When an extra was about to be taken to hospital having had an epileptic fit on set, one of her assistants was so determined to retrieve his moustache that she tried to remove it there and then. Unfortunately, it wasn't a false one. Says Samuel, 'At that point I think we realized that there are more important things in life.'

Overleaf: The 'pioneer' column sets off

Below: The make-up department had to keep track of which beards were real and which weren't ...

Chapter 8

Fire!

On 5 July 1995, just six weeks into the shoot, filming was dramatically interrupted by a massive bushfire. What follows is a vivid account of the events of that day taken from the official report by associate producer Pierre de Hinch.

The fire yesterday was within minutes of destroying the entire town of Kimberley and Lobengula's kraal. It was only an extraordinary effort by every single person on set that prevented both from being razed to the ground.

At approximately 12.00 noon I heard from the location manager that there was a fire on Nash's Farm. I immediately drove to the set in my car. On the way we phoned Bobby Duffas, who is in charge of building Lobengula's kraal, to request his help as his labour force of Zulus are experienced in fighting bushfires. Some 15 minutes later we approached the cattle-grid and drove up through the veld to the top of the hill. I saw the extent of the fire approaching the hill behind the Kimberley set. The wind was howling up the valley. Buses full of women and children who were on set as extras, trucks full of livestock, men on horseback and main unit vehicles began passing me on their way back to the base as filming had been abandoned and the set evacuated.

On reaching the Kimberley set, the fire was being diverted away from the town by volunteers from the crew, cast and extras, who had been organized into an efficient fire-fighting unit. Extras were literally beating out flames with their jackets.

I left Kimberley to go to Lobengula's kraal and on the way it became apparent that the kraal was also in imminent danger of being razed to the ground. I met Bobby Duffas and explained to him what I knew about the direction and speed of the fire and with the help of 12 of his workers he began back-burning along the road below the kraal. Within five minutes the fire had jumped the road and was heading for the kraal. More workers joined his team, desperately trying to head it off.

Meanwhile, the tents in the encampment surrounding Kimberley had caught fire, but they could be replaced...it was apparent to those still at Kimberley that the kraal was in greater danger than the town, so most people made their way across country to help Bobby and his team. For the next two hours everybody struggled to keep the fire away from the kraal, but

Left: The cast and crew battled all day to contain the fire. Below: The Kimberley set was only just saved from total devastation

back at Kimberley a stray spark had caught one of the buildings alight and within seconds it burned to the ground.

By now the fire was coming from all directions towards the kraal. Hennie Visser, the farm manager, had joined the Zulu workers in their struggle to contain the flames, as had Gavin Mey with his team from the horse department.

By now there were three fire tenders and two water bowsers helping to save the bush around the kraal. At around 3.00 p.m. air support (two helicopters and a spotter aircraft) arrived and initially began working on the adjoining game farm where farmhouses and game were in immediate danger, then began dropping water on to the fire to the north of the kraal where the fire was creeping back up the hill.

The 'airforce' continued dropping water until sunset. The Krugersdorp Fire Brigade stayed on the road near our stables until 8.00 p.m and two members of the Midrand Emergency Services stayed on the Kimberley set all night with Hennie Visser's team of farm workers.

Both Kimberley and the kraal were saved. They had taken months to build – the kraal, in particular, was irreplaceable – and the consequences for the production, had the sets burned down, were unthinkable. The Krugersdorp Fire Brigade confirmed that the fire was the largest in the area for at least five years. It was caused by two overhead cables blowing together during a storm, causing a short circuit.

July is mid-winter in South Africa, winter being the dry season, and unusual weather patterns in recent years have caused a serious drought. Bushfires are a constant hazard in the veld and the grassland at a time of drought is quite literally a tinderbox. Fire can spread faster than a man can run and can even travel underground, appearing to have been extinguished and then flaring up again elsewhere. The unusually high winds on 5 July added to the danger, fanning the fire at times into a 20-foot-high wall of flames. The fire department estimated that it was spreading at a rate of over 30 feet (around 9 metres) per second.

The day the fire broke out at Kimberley, the crew was in the middle of shooting the biggest scene of the production since filming began on 29 May. Three hundred men, women and children in period costume were on set, as well as horses, cattle, oxen, sheep and goats. Evacuating the set was the priority but extras were asked to volunteer to fight the fire. South Africans are used to bushfires and know that they can be fought effectively by beating out the flames with anything that comes to hand – in this case, their period costumes and props.

Several lives had been lost in the last fire on Nash's Farm, so no-one was in any doubt about the dangers involved in volunteering. 'The men organized themselves into fire-fighting teams, but they were literally racing from one side of the set to the other as new dangers were spotted,' says Charles Salmon, who was on his mobile phone constantly to London giving an eyewitness account of events to Scott Meek at Zenith so that he could relay the information to the BBC and the production's insurers. 'The speed of the fire and the intensity of the heat was quite terrifying. The worst thing was the smoke. We could hardly see a thing and we were all choking.'

The day was full of heroism as each and every volunteer risked their life to save the sets. People lost sight of their friends and colleagues as they were encircled by flames. At one point, Gavin Mey, the horse master, disappeared completely into the smoke. He emerged carrying a newborn calf with its umbilical cord still twisted around it – the mother had aborted in fear and fled. The calf was saved and reunited with its mother later.

On 6 July the production team returned to Nash's Farm to survey the damage. They were dismayed by what they saw. Although the main sets had been saved, the tented encampment around Kimberley and all its props had been completely destroyed, as had one of Kimberley's buildings, the governor-general's house. Thousands of acres of grassland had been burnt black and a dramatic line of scorched earth revealed how close the inferno had got to the sets. Ironically, the fire had stopped within 2 feet (just over half a metre) of the exclusive British enclave in the encampment and everything there was intact, the Union Jack still fluttering above the devastation.

The damage to the surrounding veld was extremely worrying for the producers. Previously a parched yellow, the African grassland now looked more like a blackened lunar landscape. The background view from Kimberley and the kraal had changed overnight, presenting continuity problems, and areas that had been selected for scenes in the open veld were no longer useable. But film crews are resourceful and accustomed to dealing with unforeseen circumstances. The night of the fire the schedule was adjusted, contingency plans agreed upon, and filming continued, uninterrupted, the very next day.

It was Maurice Cain who first realized the significance of the date – 5 July. It was the 142nd anniversary of Rhodes's birth. Was it coincidence – or was the spirit of Rhodes unhappy that his misdeeds were finally being told? Or, as the Zulu workers believed, was Lobengula's spirit finally avenging his downfall and the sacking of his kraal at Gubulawayo…?

Chapter 9

Zulu!

A cast of thousands

Matabele head-
dresses were
authentically
recreated for the
production

The story of Rhodes is told on an epic scale in order to re-create life in southern Africa at the end of the last century. Large numbers of people were needed to make scenes look convincingly well-populated and a total of over 900 extras were used throughout the series.

Second assistant director Adam Browne was responsible for the extras, or 'crowd'. He worked closely with casting director Christa Schamburger to ascertain the requirements on each day and liaise with the agency in Johannesburg that helped them. 'Because of the large numbers of extras who all had to be on set, dressed and made up before our main artists arrived, they often had to arrive at the base before 5.00 a.m. when it was still pitch black and freezing cold,' says Browne. 'We laid on transport from the townships, but most white extras drove their own cars to Zenex. They would then be bused to the sets on Nash's Farm, along at least two miles of rough dirt tracks. If we'd have given them a more civilized start, we would never have been ready for filming.'

He and John Watson, the first assistant director, then had the difficult task of directing the extras. Together they had to break down their inhibitions, encourage them to act convincingly without appearing self-conscious (easier said than done), prevent them from looking at the camera and remind them to take off their watches and glasses, which they somehow managed to slip back on even after being checked by the wardrobe department. 'It doesn't matter how good the principal artists are — if the background artists aren't convincing, it can spoil a scene,' says Watson. 'We were painting a huge canvas with Rhodes so the background was just as important to the overall picture as the foreground.'

Not surprisingly, many of the extras were confused and overwhelmed at finding themselves in the middle of a film set. For 99 per cent of them this was the first time, and they had little understanding of the processes involved. This confusion was exacerbated by the profusion of languages spoken in South Africa. Directions and instructions often had to be relayed in English, Afrikaans, Zulu and Xhosa.

'Sometimes the translations weren't literal,' says South African-born Browne. 'It was more a matter of getting the message across. When we were shooting the Jameson Raid in episode seven, the Afrikaner extras acting as Boer soldiers seemed a little timid and unthreatening. I said to them in Afrikaans, "Look guys, this is your last chance to annihilate the British." That got them all going.'

When Zulu extras were on set filming a scene where they were preparing for battle, they were asked to sing a war chant. Adam Browne thought he caught a few contemporary words and asked them what they were singing. It turned out that the chant was one they used to taunt the police on demonstrations in Soweto in the days of apartheid.

The Zulus who were recruited from Johannesburg for the scenes involving battles, massacres and torchings look pretty terrifying on screen. In fact, the two assistant directors had to work very hard to rouse them. Watson and Browne would demonstrate the actions required – beating someone to death, for example – while the extras would look on in bewilderment and horror. With the help of an interpreter and repeated demonstrations, the extras would become enthused. 'Once they understood what was required, and the Zulu co-ordinator had roused them by a few rounds of chanting, their energy and enthusiasm was astounding,' says John Watson. 'They would then round off a 15-hour day by singing and applauding their work.'

Making war

One of Rhodes's pivotal actions was his conquest of the Matabele tribe, who occupied the 450,000 square miles of territory north of the Transvaal and south of the Zambezi river. This land was named Rhodesia in 1894 after its conqueror, and renamed Zimbabwe in 1980 when independence was eventually achieved.

A grand indaba *(tribal conference) at the Matabele stronghold of Gubulawayo*

The Matabele had broken away from the legendary Zulu king Shaka in 1821, moved north and occupied the land of the more peaceful Shona tribe, establishing their stronghold at Gubulawayo (now Bulawayo). It was this land that Rhodes became convinced was the lost kingdom of Ophir, the legendary site of King Solomon's Mine, the source of the riches of the Queen of Sheba. The Matabele, ruled by Lobengula, stood between Rhodes and his dream of conquering land from the Cape to Cairo.

Filming this aspect of the story — Lobengula's 'court' at Gubulawayo and the bloody battles between Rhodes's 'pioneer' army and the Matabele warriors — required the participation of hundreds of Zulu extras.

The production secured the services of Barry Leitch, a renowned expert on all aspects of Zulu culture. He grew up in a village in Zululand-Natal where he spoke Zulu before he learned English. As an adult he was made an honorary Zulu, a rare privilege for a white man. He has devoted his life to recording, preserving and furthering the Zulu culture and has been involved with every film made about the Zulus since *Zulu Dawn* in 1979.

Whenever Zulu extras were required for filming, Barry Leitch and his partner Bobby Duffas, another honorary white Zulu, were constantly on set, translating and co-ordinating their participation. About a hundred of the extras came from Zululand-Natal, where the traditional culture is maintained and is part of everyday life. These were front-line extras, taking the more prominent parts in the scenes at Gubulawayo and acting as captains and lieutenants in the battle scenes. Hundreds more were recruited from hostels in Johannesburg, where blacks from the homelands live and search for casual work. Leitch and Duffas recruited these over several days. By the third day, rumours of good pay and free lunch had gone around and they were faced with a crowd of 3000 hopefuls. Those chosen spent several days with the two Zulu co-ordinators training for battle.

A 12-hour working day on *Rhodes* would yield, on average, just under four minutes of screen time. While the crew is working flat out to achieve those four minutes, the actors and extras can be hanging around for hours on end. Professional actors are used to this and have their own ways of dealing with it, but for newcomers to the world of film it can be tedious and demoralizing.

There were no such problems for the Zulu extras. In the long hours between takes they treated the crew to magnificent displays of singing, chanting, dancing and stick-fighting, their traditional male sport. They sang not simply to pass the time. Chanting and singing is an important morale-raising ritual and, before each take, Barry Leitch and Bobby Duffas would lead their chants to energize and focus them on the action to come. They considered it a great honour to take part in the filming; an opportunity to be proud of their past, to dress as warriors, to display their own culture and to re-create their history.

The big battle scene comes in episode six when the Matabele attack Rhodes's 'pioneer' army. The Matabele used the highly effective Zulu battle formation

The Matabele
massacre a Shona
village

developed by King Shaka – the *impi* – comprising a central 'chest' for frontal attack and the two 'horns' for encirclement. The Matabele attack from a high ridge, sweeping down towards the pioneer encampment (known as a 'laager'). At least half of the 400 extras were briefed to 'die' as they ran into gunfire and explosions.

After hours of rehearsal and preparation filming started. The Zulus rose up over the ridge and swarmed towards the laager, as planned. There was smoke, there was gunfire, there were explosions. There was only one problem. Not one single Zulu 'died'. They just kept running. The dismayed director called 'cut!' and the whole scene had to be re-set to start again. Duffas explained to his extras once again that when the gunfire started, they must start 'dying'.

Again, the Zulu warriors swarmed over the ridge and down the hill. And once again, not one of them 'died'. It was getting serious. Each take involved lengthy preparations by the special effects team, who had to re-set the gunfire and explosions, and on a film production, every minute counts. Bobby Duffas was dispatched to lay it on the line. He quickly got to the root of the problem. The ones that had been selected to fall were convinced that if they 'died', they wouldn't get paid. Bobby reassured them and the *impi* reassembled for yet another take. This time the warriors dropped like flies – and got straight up again. Once more, Duffas was sent into the battle lines. Now they were worried that, if they stayed on the ground, they would miss lunch.

It took a great deal of persuasion on Duffas's part to explain that, even if they 'died', they would get lunch, they would get paid, and they would be allowed to come back the next day. After that, they 'died' happily ever after.

MZILIKAZI AND THE HISTORY OF THE MATABELE NATION

Lobengula ('He That Drives Like The Wind') was born in 1833, son of Mzilikazi ('The Pathway of Blood'), founder of the Matabele nation. Mzilikazi had once been the chief induna of the legendary King Shaka, who succeeded to the Zulu chieftainship in 1816 when the Zulus numbered only 1500. But Mzilikazi became too popular for the liking of his chief and he fled from Zululand, taking his followers with him. They forged a bloody path north, over the Drakensburg mountains and into Basutoland, where they were first given the name Ndebele ('Those Who Disappear· Behind Long Shields'), known to the whites as the Matabele.

In 1839 they settled between the Limpopo and the Zambezi Rivers, securing their domination over the people of Mashonaland by a series of annual raids. They named their principal settlement in Matabeleland Gubulawayo ('The Place of the Killing').

Mzilikazi had an advisory body of indunas, and a 'royal council' of relatives. The country was divided into provinces, ruled over by his greater indunas, and sub-divided into districts that were governed by lesser indunas. His 300 wives acted as additional chiefs. Every male adult was a warrior and prisoners of war became slaves.

In 1870, the year that the young Rhodes first came to Kimberley, Mzilikazi died and he was succeeded by Lobengula. Concession hunters of all descriptions pestered him for the right to trade, dig and settle in his domain, all convinced that it was the source of the riches of King Solomon's Mines.

Lobengula tried to keep the peace but by the time Rhodes set his sights on the north, the king had his back against the wall. Yet 'the naked old savage', as Rhodes called him, always insisted on the protection of the white men who flocked to Gubulawayo. On 30 October 1888 he signed a document, written and translated to the king by the Reverend Helm, granting Rhodes exclusive rights to all the metals and minerals in his kingdom, in exchange for £100 a month, 1000 Martini-Henry rifles, 100,000 rounds of ammunition and a steamboat with guns.

It was the beginning of the end for Lobengula. He sent a deputation to Queen Victoria to verify the document he had signed, and learnt that he had been deceived. He had lost his kingdom to the white man. But still he avoided open confrontation until provoked to war by Rhodes's 'pioneers' lead by Dr Jameson in 1893. His impis, highly disciplined fighting units, were slaughtered mercilessly by the white man's Maxim machine-guns. By now suffering from smallpox, he razed Gubulawayo to the ground and fled north. He advised his people that Rhodes was their new leader and committed ritual suicide.

When Rhodes took Matabeleland, he sent Lobengula's sons to a native school and took one of them on as a valet, telling him he'd have 'No nonsense about being the son of a king'. In the 1930s there was even a Rhodes Lobengula. Today, the Ndebele make up approximately 15 per cent of the population of Zimbabwe.

Chapter 10

Horses, Battles and Hurricanes

The unsung heroes of any film or television production are the stuntmen who double for the actors if any danger is involved. No matter how fit or daring the actors are, a film's insurers simply won't allow them to endanger themselves and/or the production by doing their own stunts.

Stunts are generally thought of as dramatic fights and falls and thrilling action sequences, but British Equity, the actors' union, insists that a registered stuntman is on set when any action that could possibly be construed as dangerous is taking place. Straightforward riding, for example, requires the presence of a stunt co-ordinator. Equity's rules are so stringent that a British registered stunt co-ordinator must be on set anywhere in the world where British actors are working, to protect them from danger and to avoid massive insurance claims.

For this reason, one of Britain's most experienced stunt co-ordinators, Gerry Crampton, was hired to work alongside Gavin Mey, his South African counterpart, who was also in charge of the horse department. 'A stunt co-ordinator is what you become when you're too old or too wise to be a stuntman. I'm in charge of all the action and the safety of the actors, and I'm insured for their safety as well as my own,' says Crampton. He has doubled for an impressive list of stars, including Jack Nicholson, Charles Bronson, Lee Marvin, Michael Caine, Sean Connery and Kirk Douglas (with whom he worked for 12 years). After 50 years of taking risks on behalf of others, he has been in hospital three times, lost half a testicle in a motorbike stunt and had a steel plate in his head for nine months.

Horses, horses, everywhere...

Most of the action on *Rhodes* involved horses, as horseback, or horsedrawn vehicles, were the only method of transport at that time. The actors had to learn to ride, drive waggons and gallop headlong into battle, guns blazing. Almost every exterior scene involved horses, and even in interior scenes horses were often required to pass by windows or open doors.

RHODES

Such were the equine demands of the production that a horse department was required. Stables on the edge of Nash's Farm were set up and 48 horses were bought and permanently stabled with horse master Gavin Mey. However, even they had to be auditioned to ensure that the horses ridden by the leading actors were compatible. Rather like humans, some horses simply don't like each other and certainly wouldn't share a scene with a rival. There are prima donnas in the horse world, too! For really big scenes, such as the assembling of Rhodes's 'pioneer' army, extra horses and riders were provided by the local mounted police.

The stables became a training centre for actors, who were flown to South Africa several weeks ahead of their filming dates. In Rhodes's time, horses were ridden Western-style, with the rider using only his reins to control the horse, rather than a bit. Even for actors with some experience of riding, the loose-reined technique is quite a challenge, requiring great confidence and considerable skill. After time spent building confidence in the paddock, the actors were taken into the open veld where their riding experience really began. With uninterrupted African landscape and rolling hills as far as the eye could see, it was every fantasy cowboy's dream come true.

Training wasn't confined just to the actors. The horses all underwent an intensive programme, too. Although they were used to being ridden, most weren't used to being driven. For the production they had to pull carts, waggons, coaches and gun-carriages, which required special training. As well as that, they had to be taught to cope with pandemonium going on all around them, rather like police horses.

Dr Jameson (Neil Pearson) leads the 'pioneer' column

'Horses are so highly strung and unpredictable, you never know what's going to frighten them,' explains Gavin Mey. 'We got them used gradually to explosions, flashes of light and guns going off around them. But even then, they could be frightened by something quite unexpected. Horses are just like people – they all have their individual foibles. One of our horses was fine with explosions, but terrified of cola cans. Film sets are always crawling with electric cables and these often frighten horses because they think they are snakes.'

Even with Gavin Mey's insight into horse psychology, there were still a few problems. 'We were shooting the scene where the 'pioneer' army, led by Jameson, crosses the Vaal river and the Matabele warriors first show themselves. Our main worry was the safety and viability of the horses crossing the river. They were already unsettled by the flat, rocky surface approaching the river, which they didn't like, even though we'd done several trial runs,' Mey recalls. 'Then the Matabele warriors appeared. With their huge feather headdresses they looked like giants. The horses took one look, didn't like what they saw, and made for home. We hadn't foreseen that one!'

As Neil Pearson, who plays Dr Jameson, commented later, 'How would you feel if you saw a 6-foot chicken coming straight for you?'

Taking horses into battle was another thing altogether. They had to be trained to charge into action, with gunfire and explosions going off all around. They also had to be trained to fall at the gallop. 'It takes six weeks to train a horse to fall at the gallop, from standing to walking and eventually to galloping,' explains Gerry Crampton. 'We start with a straw bed to practise on and we have to do it every day. People worry about cruelty and whether we use trip wires, but I can assure you it's all done with kindness.' He points out that 'Horses have good memories – if they have to do something they don't like, they won't do it again. In filming we have to do everything over and over again, so if they weren't happy, we'd be sunk.'

Just as the actors had to be transported to the location, made up and dressed, then fed and watered all day, so did the horses. The time they were needed on set had to be scheduled, and if the location were within riding distance of the stables, they would be ridden or brought in a column by Gavin Mey's team of riders and grooms. If the location was further afield, they would often have to set off the night before, and if they were being ridden in a column on Nash's Farm, their precise time of departure from the stables would be planned so that they would not hold up the convoy of unit vehicles which would inevitably be trundling along the rocky tracks like some bizarre circus.

Even well-trained horses can be unpredictable and headstrong, and despite their intensive riding lessons, the actors were still relatively inexperienced in the saddle. On one particularly frustrating occasion towards the end of an exhausting and relentlessly hot day, two actors had to ride off into the distance, along a dirt track. Time and time again, they galloped away and veered off the track in the wrong direction. After the sixth take, director David Drury was heard to scream, 'Will somebody find me a horse that works!'

SPECIAL EFFECTS

Special effects are an integral part of any big action sequence on film. The special effects supervisor looks after the mechanics of stunts, planning, executing and overseeing anything from fires, explosions and floods to gunfire, battles and hurricanes. He is responsible for achieving a dramatic effect on screen, while ensuring the safety of all those involved.

British special effects supremo Ken Lailey worked closely with his South African counterpart, Max Poolman, to achieve some spectacular action in *Rhodes*. Two of the biggest scenes requiring special effects (SFX) are the tornado hitting Kimberley in episode one and the Matabele battle in episode six.

The tornado

The first of these scenes is set in 1872, when a tornado hits the diamond diggings and the nearby town of Kimberley. Young Rhodes is at the mine when the tornado strikes and does what he can to secure equipment before taking shelter in Kimberley's London Hotel. To his disgust, he finds his brother Herbert drunk and oblivious to the devastation being wreaked by the storm.

Ordinary wind machines were not powerful enough to simulate the effect of a tornado, so a low-level helicopter was used to create a moving wall of dust over the diamond diggings. At Kimberley, where it wasn't practical to use a helicopter, the production borrowed a commercial aircraft engine on a stationary test-bed. Combined with four huge wind machines and hundreds of tons of Fuller's Earth, it had the desired effect.

The SFX team had spent days carefully rigging the buildings of Kimberley so that they would be 'ripped apart' by the tornado, creating water towers that would totter and fall and fixing sides of buildings to be torn off by the wind.

When it came time to filming, conditions for cast and crew were extremely unpleasant. The roar of the aircraft engine was deafening and the fine dust permeated everything – hair, nose, throat and cameras.

It was also, potentially, a dangerous day on set. Everybody had been warned about the risks of aircraft propellers, wind machines, stampeding cattle and falling debris, but in the event, an accident that no-one had foreseen occurred. While filming a scene when the young Rhodes and Christmas, his manservant, run towards the London Hotel and bang on the door to be let in, Joe Shaw hammered rather too vigorously. The glass shattered and a shard embedded itself in his arm. He was whisked off to hospital in Johannesburg while the team continued shooting other aspects of the scene. He returned later in the day, having been given a tetanus injection and the all-clear. For the rest of the scene, he wore a ragged bandage around his forearm – thought more appropriate to the period than a sticking plaster – and Patrick Shai (Christmas) did the hammering on the door.

RHODES

The battle

In episode six, set in 1893, Rhodes's 'pioneer' army, led by Dr Jameson, invades Lobengula's territory and pitches camp in a dry river valley. At dawn, the Matabele army swarms over the hillside and attacks the laager. Rhodes's men fend off the attack with Maxim machine guns, slaughtering hundreds of Lobengula's warriors, powerless against the might of the new automatic weapons. They had rejected guns in favour of their traditional assegai (short stabbing spears), believing it was unmanly to fight at long range. This belief proved to be their downfall.

South African armourer Bruce Wentzel supplied the guns for the scene and was responsible for loading the rifles and instructing the actors how to handle them. Over 140 firing weapons were used in the scene, plus the Maxim machine guns. The original Maxims are all in museums, so exact copies were created for the production that could actually be fired using special blanks. 'With normal blanks there is always some discharge and some element of risk,' explains Charles Salmon. 'We use a special blank which can be fired at extremely close range and looks convincing, but is no danger at all to the actor using the gun, or anyone in the vicinity.'

The big battle sequence in episode six took three days to film

At the other end of the gunfire, the bullet hits and explosions are all meticulously prepared beforehand. 'All the machine-gun hits from the laager are laid on the ground in a line of twelve that fire in sequence in order to give the effect of machine-gun fire,' explains Ken Lailey. 'We use a cork block with a squib – a little electric detonator – in it. On each cork block is a handful of Fuller's Earth, which creates debris and gives the visual effect of an explosion.' The same process was used to create the effect of bullets hitting Matabele shields. Again, each squib had to be carefully placed in the shields before the scene was shot.

The explosions were then triggered by a team of experienced special-effects men from a long-range vantage point. As the Matabele swarm down the hillside amid gunfire and explosions, the effect is one of the genuine chaos of battle. This relies on the expertise of Ken Lailey and his team, and on the experienced Zulu stuntmen who head the action. Max Poolman, the South African SFX co-ordinator, paid tribute to Ken Lailey: 'The types of effects that we're using on this production are fairly new here, but we're all keen to learn. The British are known to be the best special-effects men in the world.'

Chapter 11

The Actors' Perspective

THE WOMAN
WHO DESTROYED RHODES

In his day Cecil Rhodes was reputed to be a 'woman-hater'. He may not have actually hated women, but he certainly moved in exclusively male circles, surrounding himself with loyal business partners and a coterie of attractive young men. Only one woman penetrated this circle successfully – a woman who was to have a devastating effect on his life. Frances Barber, who plays Princess Catherine Radziwill, found out as much as she could about the extraordinary Russian aristocrat. This is her view of the woman who literally hounded Rhodes to death.

I found out as much as I could about the princess but her background is somewhat ambiguous as she was continually re-inventing herself. What is known is that she was from a well-to-do family in rural Russia, that she married a Polish count and that she moved to Berlin, where she was expected to embrace German court life – which for women involved embroidery, playing the piano, and hosting dinner parties. This sounds fine to me, but the princess was a bit of a maverick, a free spirit who loved adventure. She visited an aunt in Paris and was much taken with the Parisian way of life. Back in Berlin she livened things up by starting scurrilous rumours and publishing a diary revealing the secrets of court life under a pseudonym. She was ostracized under suspicion of being the author and forced to leave the country. Today it would be the equivalent of a servant at Buckingham Palace selling stories to the tabloid press – except this was even more shocking, because she was a member of the aristocracy. Rasputin-like rumours spread around her – she was thought to be more politically dangerous than she probably was. Nevertheless, she enjoyed exploiting this myth.

Frances Barber plays Princess Catherine Radziwill

In her late 30s she came to London where she used her royal title to move in the right circles and meet the right people. When she met Cecil Rhodes in 1899 she was immediately attracted by his ruthlessness and ambition. I don't believe she was ever interested in a love affair. She responded to his power and charisma, and the sheer audacity with which he had colonized a massive continent.

She very quickly recognized that Rhodes would not be interested in her sexually. When she proposed marriage she actually said, 'I will free you from any matrimonial demands which might conflict with your nature'. It's difficult nowadays to appreciate quite how astonishing it was that she even recognized his sexual preference, let alone refer to it. Homosexuality was not really acknowledged in those days — and certainly not mentioned openly in polite society. To me this shows what an extraordinary woman she was — so far ahead of her time.

Far from being shocked or disturbed by Rhodes's sexuality, she thought it would serve her cause. Marriage would legitimize his bachelorhood. As a married couple they would have been impregnable, and she simply couldn't believe that Rhodes would reject such an expedient offer.

I think she then became obsessed with the notion of marrying him, of becoming a partner in his great enterprise to extend the British Empire from the Cape to Cairo. I don't believe she ever set out to destroy him but when he refused her offer, her frustration drove her to desperate measures. She gathered more and more ammunition against him, convinced that he would finally capitulate.

You might say that the princess personifies the saying, 'Hell hath no fury like a woman scorned'. But her fury wasn't the result of a broken heart. She was furious that he was rejecting the opportunity to paint Africa British red with her at his side. She felt that he was abandoning his dream of world domination — if anything she was even more ambitious than he was. She shared his ideals and his lust for power.

I think Rhodes was initially intrigued by her. She was so much more worldly-wise than the Home Counties Englishwomen he was used to. But when she got too close he must have been terrified. He was from a staunch, starch-shirted, stiff-upper-lip English background. He simply couldn't combat her honesty or daring. He couldn't hoist her or humiliate her by suggesting that she was behaving dishonourably or letting the side down. She was shocking, remarkable and unstoppable. Rhodes could stop most people in his tracks with a sudden explosion of temper or by using his renowned charm. But whatever he tried, she had another move on the chessboard. She was completely fearless, and just as manipulative and determined as he was.

In many ways she reminds me of Mrs Thatcher — she was an unstoppable force who wore down or ignored the opposition. There are very few women in history whose driving force is the pursuit of power, rather than love. The princess is definitely one of them. Like Rhodes, her passion was Africa, and she was prepared to destroy anything that stood in her path.

She served a prison sentence for repeatedly forging Rhodes's signature in an attempt to expose his misdemeanours and crimes in a public trial, but little is known of her after that except that she died alone in New York in 1941, aged 84. I admire her hugely for her chutzpah, her independence and modernity. She was a unique character in her time and it seems sad that she didn't achieve more.

NEIL PEARSON TAKES UP THE REINS

Neil Pearson plays Dr Jameson, the surgeon-turned-soldier who became one of Rhodes's closest friends and allies. Rhodes flattered him into believing he was an empire-builder, but ultimately Jameson's recklessness brought disgrace and imprisonment. Because of the quirks of the filming schedule, Pearson spent longer in South Africa than any of the other British actors. This is his version of his six-month stay.

Step one, as always: get the job. Someone had already been cast as Jameson, which would usually be a drawback, but he was offered a great big American movie and pulled out at the last minute. As it turned out, the movie never got made, and I spent six months in South Africa on the job of a lifetime ... but I'm not one to laugh myself sick at the misfortunes of others. (Never be too proud to accept parts turned down by other people: there are only three actors in the world who are first choice for anything, and that's only when the other two are busy.)

The producers sent me the scripts, all 10 hours of them, and gave me three hours to make a decision. They seemed desperate. When I found they were offering me the part of a short, bald, brown-eyed, Zulu-speaking, horse-riding doctor from Edinburgh, they seemed even more desperate. But the scripts were very good, Martin Shaw was playing Rhodes and I'd never been to South Africa before. I said yes.

My first meeting with Cecil Rhodes took place at Zenith's offices in London, where the British actors had been invited to meet each other. I'd been cast only a week before, and felt a tad under-prepared. Martin was already there when I arrived, sitting at the table surrounded by biographies and reference books which the bastard gave every impression of having read. And he'd already grown the moustache. He was warmly welcoming and sufficiently confident of his own ability not to feel threatened by other people's ideas. Not that I had any. Joe Shaw had just left drama school, and this was his first job. He, too, was alarmingly well-researched, and was trying not to look either (a) as happy as a dog with two dicks, or (b) terrified. Then Ken Stott, who plays Barney Barnato, shambled in. Stott is always doing about six jobs at once and, comfortingly, had the air of not being sure which one this meeting was about. I began to feel better.

We settled down to wait for Frances Barber. People spend a lot of time waiting for Frances Barber. They do this because she is invariably worth the wait. She eventually descended in a blur of apologies, perfume and shopping bags. Delving into one of the bags, she heaved the scripts — all eight of them — onto the table, apparently under the impression that we were about to embark on a ten-hour read-through. Frances would have made Neville Chamberlain feel well-informed. Thus assembled, this cream of British talent, and me, was addressed by Scott Meek, the show's producer. My mission, apparently, was to go out to South Africa two months before I was required for shooting and learn to ride a horse.

Johannesburg is not the prettiest city in the world. It's not even the second prettiest. Like Los Angeles, it is geometrically laid out and crime-ridden. Also like Los Angeles, it has no heart, geographical or otherwise. And it is infested with shopping malls. (If you want to kill a city stone dead, build shopping malls.) In downtown Johannesburg, the Market Theatre now stands in sheepish isolation amid blocks of unloved buildings and undeveloped land. It looks embarrassed, like it's been stood up. The unused sites have become ad hoc car parks and, if you're very, very lucky, your car will still be there when you come back. I spent as little time in the city as I could.

I wasn't involved in the first seven weeks of filming. Martin and Ken were off doing things I know about — rehearsals, costume fittings, filming. You know, acting. The rest of us were told to report to a farm an hour's drive from Johannesburg. If you ever decide to learn to ride, do it at someone else's expense in the middle of a great big South African nowhere. The sun will beat down on you, ochre dust will rise from hooves, and your instructors will look like refugees from a Marlboro ad. You will arrive for your first lesson looking terrified, then they will kit you out in a riding hat and breeches that will make you look terrified and ridiculous. But you will have fun.

Joe had a lot of natural talent, but very little confidence. I, on the other hand, had bags of confidence and no natural talent whatsoever. We had to learn to ride Western style. This involves sitting so low in the saddle that all your vertebrae collect in your skull, and holding both reins in the left hand so that you can shoot people with your right. After several lessons and extensive physiotherapy we were led out of the corral for the first time. A mile or so away lay the main set: the town of Kimberley, circa 1870, had risen again courtesy of the art department, and seven of us rode into town.

It was my first look at the place, and only then did the scale of the series begin to sink in. No chipboard facades for us. These were real buildings for filming inside and out, all set against a background of untouched landscape that stopped your heart; television on a scale everyone said was no longer possible. As we moseyed down the dusty main street, someone suggested we call ourselves 'The Magnificent Seven'. We settled for 'The Mild Bunch'.

I'd now been in South Africa two months. I'd learned to ride, I'd been to Durban to watch the Rugby World Cup, I'd spent a weekend in Sun City (Blackpool with carpets — fine by me, I like Blackpool), and I'd watched more Grade Z videos than flesh and blood could stand. But I hadn't actually filmed anything. Martin and Ken had been shooting scene after scene in smoke-filled rooms, Joe had started filming Rhodes's early days of derring-do. The word from the set was very good. I began to feel a bit of a gooseberry.

So I learnt some Zulu. I had a dozen or so lines in Zulu and I was sent off to a tutor to polish them up. Zulu is a

Neil Pearson
as Dr Jameson

beautiful language when spoken by Zulus; I sounded like I was having a seizure. It's a 'click' language: there are five or so different clicks that are made with different parts of the mouth, tongue, teeth, palate, whatever. (Do not attempt to speak Zulu if you wear dentures: someone could get hurt.) Jameson had been an atrocious Zulu speaker and I was able to bring this part of him to life superbly well.

My first day of filming finally arrived and that night I went out with Ken to celebrate. He was celebrating having finished, I was celebrating having said my first line. By the time I finished 'Rhodes' Ken had gone on to make a four-part series for the BBC.

At long last it was time to shoot the action scenes that involved me and my horse. They're very big, horses. Put a hundred or so in one place and things can get out of hand. August was spent shooting all the set pieces: battles, encampments, river crossings. Now I felt involved. I could ride, my moustache was in fine fettle (we all had to grow them — out of costume we looked like a reunion of the Village People), and I was working every day.

But the filming wasn't without its ironies. Here we were in the new South Africa and all the whites — South African and English actors backed up by extras from the South African Mounted Police — were dressed in colonial uniforms. All the black actors and extras were dressed as late-19th-century Zulus, and we would spend each working day killing them. It felt a little…odd.

Everyone in South Africa knows they've been invited to a party, but no-one's quite sure if it's black tie or fancy dress. The economic apartheid is as entrenched as it ever was, and now that the have-nots can see more clearly what the haves have got, crime has gone through the roof (or, more accurately, across the garden in the middle of the night and through a side window). But for all its problems, it remains a place of great optimism. Most surprisingly, there is no sense of vengefulness: within a year of taking power, the Government had abolished the death penalty. Just when judicial revenge might have been expected to become the order of the day, Mandela's Government dismantled the apparatus that made it possible. After 27 years in prison, Mandela took office and made reconciliation his watchword, thereby denying anybody in South Africa the moral authority to call for an eye for an eye.

I was invited to a rally being addressed by Mandela. The first council elections were being held, and the president was out on the stump for the ANC. I imagined I would be going to a 100 000-seater stadium to listen to a little brown speck through a bad PA system. I found myself in a local village hall in an audience of a few hundred. Mandela spoke for an hour-and-a-half, without notes. For the first 45 minutes I sat thinking, 'Christ, that's Nelson Mandela'. For the second 45 minutes I sat thinking, 'Christ, I could murder a pizza'. Normality is coming to South Africa very quickly: local politics there are about as interesting as...local politics anywhere else.

Filming moved through September and the more I shot, the happier I felt. I fell off my horse into a river (mercifully not on camera) and found that the wranglers took me far more seriously as a horseman once I'd been pitched on my arse. More and more of the actors were finishing filming, and individual wrap parties became almost nightly occurrences. South Africa had won the Rugby World Cup months ago, and now the England cricket team was arriving for a hammering. Stott and Shaw Jnr had long since gone home. Frances Barber was yet to arrive (no change there, then). And on it went...

I finished in late October, two weeks before the final wrap. A party was thrown at Zenith for the other early finishers (most of the cast), and so the job ended where it had begun. A six-month round-trip. As I write, I've not yet seen a frame of it, but I doubt you'll see a more convincing short, bald, brown-eyed, Zulu-speaking, horse-riding doctor on your screens all year.

A VIEW FROM SOUTH AFRICA

South African actor Gavin Hood plays the mercenary soldier Frank Johnson, who was unexpectedly chosen by Rhodes to recruit and lead his 'pioneer' army northwards in Africa. Hood is a well-known face in his home country, following his starring role in a popular, long-running South African television series, *The Game*, which chronicled the friendship between two rugby players – one white and one Coloured.

He could not have been more surprised to learn that he was being offered a part in South Africa's biggest-ever television production – mainly because he had left South Africa only three weeks earlier, taking up residence in London where he was planning to pursue his career as a screenwriter. He had no qualms, however, about taking a break from writing to film *Rhodes*.

He believes that the shooting of the series in South Africa and the involvement of the South African Broadcasting Corporation is an important step in the cultural development of the new country. Television was not introduced into South Africa until 1976, when Hood was 13. 'When television arrived we were suddenly bombarded with American culture. I notice how Americanized the younger generation of South Africans are. I think this bombardment, this swamping with US product, creates a crisis of identity and a sense of inferiority. It's not good for a country trying to find its feet, seeking to establish a new identity. An absence of drama that deals with one's own experiences and dilemmas can leave individuals feeling alienated and I think this is a big problem in South Africa. We all need the opportunity to reflect on our own past.'

Because of international boycotts during the years of apartheid, South Africa was largely culturally isolated from the rest of the world. Gavin Hood has strong feelings about the wisdom of such wide-ranging sanctions. 'I have no doubt that the changes in South Africa were largely precipitated by economic sanctions, but I don't believe that cultural sanctions are ever a good idea. A country is brought to its knees by economic sanctions, by trade and arms embargoes. But when you prevent cultural exchange you either make way for something else – which in South Africa's case was American values – or you leave a vacuum for the ruling regime to expound its own propaganda. People don't have any other points of reference and the ruling regime then has total control.'

He is only too aware of the cultural complexity of growing up in South Africa. 'I am a white, English-speaking South African with an English colonial background. My grandparents came to South Africa before the Second World War and I have aunts and uncles in England. I was brought up with an English heritage, with English literary and theatrical traditions. We read and recited Shakespeare at school. I grew thinking I was English, yet not being exposed to current English culture because of the economic and cultural boycott. It was like being in a suspended time zone.'

Despite his English heritage, Hood is first and foremost a South African. 'I am incredibly proud of the way we are trying to come to terms with our past and forge a new future,' he says. 'We South Africans have a complicated history and we live in a terribly exciting present. We live with hope and fear. We live with passion, anger, excitement, resentment, guilt. We have 11 official languages. We are black, we are white, and all the colours in between. We need to see our complexity and diversity reflected in our film and television. I think *Rhodes* is a fine example of a project that gives South Africans and Britons a chance to reflect on their history, and at the same time be well entertained.'

He hopes that there will be more stories seen on screens around the world that reflect on the South African experience, both past and present. 'South Africa has a great deal to offer the world of film and television because it's a country of extremes. Its dilemmas and issues have international significance and they bring a vitality to subjects that you don't find in more stable environment.'

Opposite: Gavin Hood as Frank Johnson

Chapter 12

Music and Post-Production

The music for *Rhodes* is a unique and evocative mix of Western orchestral music and traditional Zulu vocal music. The orchestral score was specially composed by Alan Parker and the Zulu music was recorded during an extraordinary visit to Zululand-Natal in October 1995 by the series' music producer, Graham Walker, and his co-ordinator, Liz Schrek.

Zulu music

Graham Walker and Liz Schrek travelled to Simunye in Natal to record the Zulus' traditional songs and chants. Simunye, which has no running water or electricity and is a mile from the nearest road, is the home village of Barry Leitch, the series' Zulu advisor. Men, women and children came from villages for miles around, travelling for several hours on foot and horseback to perform for them.

Music is an essential part of Zulu culture. Through songs and chants passed down through generations they tell their history, celebrate important occasions, express their emotions, lift their spirits, and inspire themselves for battle or difficult tasks. For Graham Walker they performed war chants, love songs, wedding songs and funeral songs, all of which would be used throughout the series. 'It was a life-changing and deeply moving experience,' he says.

Walker and Schrek recorded 11 hours of music. At the end of their stay they were honoured by a visit from the Zulu chief, Prince Gelengi Biyela (He Who Roars Like a Bull), now in his 90s, whose grandfather fought against the British in the Zulu war of 1879. They were introduced to him as 'Queen Victoria's people from across the water'. He spoke of the treachery of the British politicians and of the bravery of the British soldiers. His warriors still wear tartan kilts on certain ceremonial occasions as a tribute to the fighting spirit of the British soldier.

Barry Leitch advised Graham Walker on the etiquette of meeting the prince. He told him his head should never be higher than the prince's, so when the Zulu chief sat down, Graham should sit down even faster. Leitch recommended presenting the chief with a goat, to thank him for allowing him to use the music of his people. A huge goat with long horns was brought into the hut for Graham to make his presentation. To his horror, the chief responded by handing him a large ceremonial knife, indicating that he should slit the goat's throat. Feeling a little queasy, Graham thrust the goat towards the chief saying, 'May you and the goat have a long and happy life' and hoping that this message would lose nothing in the translation. To his mighty relief, the prince split his sides laughing. It had all been a big joke – the goat was to join the royal herd.

The prince explained that he would take the goat back to his village and would tell his people, and his forefathers, that he spoke to the white man and that this is the wonderful thanks that he received. As his people live in villages for miles around, he would roar the news from a hilltop in chants that would be incorporated into his tribe's folklore. 'It is very important that these stories are handed down to the young and to those that are yet to be born,' he explained.

Orchestral music

The original orchestral music in the series was composed by Alan Parker, after lengthy discussions with director David Drury at the post-production stage. There are between four and five hours of music in the series. 'Alan came up with a terrific score – a wonderful mix of ethnic and Western music,' says Graham Walker. 'The orchestral music was inspired by music of the British Empire, which blends beautifully with the traditional Zulu vocal songs and chants. There are several recurring themes, including the title theme, which explodes into contemporary rhythms for the montage of shots from present-day Johannesburg at the climax of the series. The orchestral music was recorded in 14 three-hour sessions using a range of musicians, from a full orchestra of 70 to small ensembles of 16.' The music is all performed by the London Metropolitan Orchestra, with well-known international soloists led by the renowned violinist Jonathan Reece.

Source music

Music is an integral element of certain scenes, such as a military parade, a dance or a concert. This non-original 'source' music was researched and recorded before filming began, so that it could be incorporated into the scene while filming. For these, Graham Walker carefully researched the music of the time – waltzes, popular songs, military music, chamber music. He went to Knellar Hall in Twickenham, to the Royal School of Military Music, where he trained as a musician in the Royal Tank Regiment. He also consulted the Gilbert and Sullivan Society and the British Reference Library to trace music that would be correct for the period and to ensure that the music would have been available in Africa in Rhodes's day. This music was pre-recorded in England before the shoot in South Africa, and took seven three-hour recording sessions.

Post-production

The longest process in the production of *Rhodes* was what is known as post-production, which was overseen by Chris Catterall and Mike Nunn. Post-production is a general term for the various technical stages involved in editing the pictures and sound, adding music, titles and any visual and sound effects, and blending and refining the combined elements to achieve the finished product.

One might imagine that post-production starts as soon as production finishes. In fact, post-production begins on the second day of filming. On *Rhodes*, the film from each day's shoot was couriered by air back to London to be processed at Rank Film Laboratories overnight. These 'rushes' or 'dailies' were transferred to tape, copies were made and returned immediately to South Africa for viewing by the producer and director.

The military music in the series was researched by Graham Weller and recorded before filming began

Editing

Tucked away in his editing suite at Shepperton Studios, editor Ian Farr started to assemble the material as soon as it arrived from the first day's filming. Because the whole series was shot out of order, it was like working on a massive jigsaw with only a few pieces from totally different sections. For example, one particular scene from episode one wasn't shot until the very last day of filming. Gradually, more and more of the missing pieces came in and the whole picture was complete.

By the time director David Drury had finished shooting in South Africa and returned to England, Ian Farr had roughly assembled all eight episodes. This was a working assembly for Drury, who spent two weeks on each episode, putting his stamp on the edit by deciding which takes to use and how to make the best possible use of the material. This version, the 'director's cut', was sent to the producers and financiers for their approval.

Music spotting

Once the director's cut was approved and any further changes had been made, David Drury viewed the final cut with music producer Graham Walker and composer Alan Parker to identify the music requirements – the exact moments where background music would enhance the drama or atmosphere. This process is known as 'music spotting'. Parker then began composing the original music, including the title themes. Once written, it was recorded with the composer conducting the musicians in synchronization with the picture.

Post-synching

No matter how careful the sound recordist is during filming, there are always occasions when background noise, weather conditions or the action in the scene make it impossible to record dialogue clearly. These scenes require a process known as ADR – Audio Dialogue Re-recording, or post-synching (i.e. synchronization). The actors are brought to a specialized ADR theatre to re-record their lines standing in front of the scene and attempting to match their words to the picture.

Dubbing

With the final content of the series assembled and agreed, the four sound editors were brought in to even out and blend all the soundtracks, a process known as dubbing. They overlaid background noise to enhance atmosphere and ensure that the sound of a scene ran smoothly and added in the music and special sound effects. Ironically, a sound editor has done a good job if his or her work is never noticed. The aim is to make the sound so natural and complementary to the images that it never stands out.

The final dubbing mix balances all aspects of the sound – originally recorded dialogue, re-recorded dialogue, music, background sound and special effects.

Grading

This is the final stage of post-production. Until now, all the work had been done electronically on tape – a far cry from the days when editors literally cut the film by hand. Only now do the technicians return to the original negative to cut it. The newly assembled negative is graded, so that the colour and contrast are balanced, and the final picture is of a consistent quality.

Finally, the dubbed soundtrack was combined with the graded picture, credits and titles and the show was at long last ready for transmission. The post-production of *Rhodes*, from the start of shoot to the final delivery of all eight episodes, took 15 months.

Overleaf: The sun
sets over
Nash's Farm

Chapter 13

Series Guide

EPISODE ONE: ALL THE WORLD'S DIAMONDS

In 1899, Cecil John Rhodes is honoured at Oxford as the new British hero, empire-builder, the Colossus of Africa. At the age of 45 he controls the world's diamonds and a country almost the size of Europe bears his name — Rhodesia. He is also the world's most eligible bachelor. Princess Catherine Radziwill, an exotic Russian aristocrat, is drawn to Rhodes. His cool manner only excites her curiosity. She follows him back to Cape Town and charms her way into his inner circle. There he tells her about his past. It began in 1871...

The young Rhodes, dressed in cricket flannels and school blazer, travels with his manservant, Christmas, across the African veld. They are heading for the vast new diamond mines that have opened up 500 miles north of Cape Town, where his brother Herbert is trying his luck as a diamond prospector.

Aged only 18 and in delicate health, Rhodes has come prepared with lists of diamond prices and journals on excavating machinery. They arrive at New Rush, the squalid shanty town that has sprung up near the mines where outlaws from every continent live cheek-by-jowl with African tribesmen.

Rhodes is unimpressed with Herbert's friends and finds he has more in common with John Merriman, a member of the Cape Parliament. Rhodes quickly realizes that the mines should be mechanized and shares his ideas with Merriman. He introduces a pulley system to one of Herbert's claims and starts working unflinchingly, watched admiringly by his neighbour, Rudd.

Rhodes explains to Merriman that the value of diamonds rests in their rarity. Therefore, the supply of diamonds should be controlled to keep prices high. He is already making money and out-manoeuvring the wily diamond dealers.

When a tornado hits New Rush the diggings are badly damaged. The black workers start to flee but Rhodes persuades them to stay by taking the unprecedented step of paying them in advance. Other prospectors are horrified, but Rhodes already understands the importance of trust in African culture. He shares his workers with Rudd, insisting that they are to be treated honourably.

Herbert leaves to seek his fortune further north in the gold fields and signs his claims over to Rhodes. But it is a difficult time. Prices are falling and the weakened diggings regularly cave in. When the road between their claims collapses, Rhodes and Rudd decide to join forces.

Alyward, an Ulsterman and rabble-rouser, provokes unrest among the diggers by accusing the blacks of prospering at the whites' expense. He insists that blacks should be prevented from owning claims and incites the diggers to smash black claims and round up the workers into a compound.

Alyward is about to whip a black worker for stealing diamonds when Rhodes intervenes, claiming that illegal white buyers, not black workers, are the source of the trouble. His theory is proved correct and the black worker is released.

Britain annexes the diamond territory and New Rush is renamed Kimberley. Sir Richard Southey is the new governor-general. Rhodes quickly makes an impression on Southey and his entourage. He appeals to Southey to allow amalgamation of the claims but the views of a mere 19-year old are disregarded. Prices fall, as Rhodes predicts, and he and Rudd buy as many claims as they can, realizing that the main source of the diamonds is still untapped.

Ownership of claims is still restricted and, frustrated, Rhodes returns to England to fulfil his first ambition – to study at Oxford. There he is seized by a second, far greater, ambition. Inspired by a speech by the high priest of Victorian Imperialism, John Ruskin, Rhodes decides that he will take Africa for the English race – and diamonds will give him the means. However, two obstacles stand in his way. He suffers a massive heart attack and is given only six months to live. He

Young Rhodes persuades his workers to stay on after the tornado

returns to Kimberley and tells Merriman that the rest of his life is a race against time. The second obstacle is Barney Barnato, a brash cockney Jew newly arrived in Kimberley, who is soon to become Rhodes's greatest rival.

By now the other prospectors have emulated Rhodes and their diggings too are mechanized. Rhodes secretly sabotages their pumps, thereby securing the profitable pumping contract for the whole De Beers mine.

Sir Richard Southey has been dismissed for being too liberal and Rhodes is publicly accused of sabotage. He uses his influence to get himself off the hook.

Rhodes meets Alfred Beit, a successful Jewish diamond-buyer. Beit's ambition is to control the world's diamonds. He and Rhodes clearly have a great deal in common.

EPISODE TWO: ALL THE WORLD'S GOLD

By 1880, Barney Barnato has bought the richest claims in the Kimberley mine. When he opens a public company, Rhodes responds by launching the De Beers Mining Company, but he is a long way from owning all the claims at the De Beers mine.

Neville Pickering, a young trainee clerk, catches the attention of Rhodes. He appoints Pickering to run De Beers while he concentrates on his political career. He intends to stand for election to the Cape Parliament.

In 1881, Rhodes takes his seat in the Cape Parliament as the new member for Barkly West and is introduced to Sir Hercules Robinson, who has taken over the post of governor-general.

Rhodes secretly buys a newspaper, the *Cape Argus*, despite his old friend Merriman's warning of rumours that Rhodes is buying favours and influence. Rhodes is trying to woo the Boers, who want to force the natives into slavery, which goes against Merriman's more liberal views.

Twenty years later Merriman is known to be a bitter enemy of Rhodes. The princess visits him and offers to mediate between them, claiming that she and Rhodes are engaged to be married. She asks Merriman to explain why they became such bitter enemies. Merriman takes up the story...

Rhodes persuades young Pickering to move in to his humble cottage in Kimberley. When Rhodes is summoned urgently to Cape Town, he gives Pickering an envelope leaving everything to him in trust.

Sir Hercules Robinson tells Rhodes that the British Government is giving Bechuanaland to the natives. Rhodes insists that it is Britain's road to the African interior and it must be kept open. Rhodes speaks in Parliament and shocks Merriman by declaring that natives should be denied the vote and that despotism should be supported.

This change of attitude in Rhodes forces his faithful manservant, Christmas, to leave him. Even with bribery, Rhodes is unable to persuade him to stay.

Rhodes and Pickering host a grand dance at the newly founded Kimberley Club and Rhodes looks on jealously as his young friend enjoys dancing with the ladies. The powerful diamond-buyer Alfred Beit reminds Rhodes that, despite the name of his new company, he does not yet own the whole De Beers mine.

There is an emergency at the De Beers mine, where black workers are now kept in a compound. Several cases of smallpox have broken out. Rhodes realizes that an epidemic could close the mine.

When Pickering is badly injured in a riding accident, Rhodes befriends the local doctor, Jameson, who treats the septicaemia that develops. Still fearful that the De Beers mine will be closed because of smallpox, Rhodes persuades his new friend to conceal the risk of an epidemic. When the cover-up is revealed, Merriman exposes Rhodes in Parliament and becomes one of his most vehement opponents.

Pickering recovers slowly and takes his seat on the board of De Beers along with Alfred Beit. Rhodes and Beit scheme to take over other companies and extend their control of the diamond market.

When gold is discovered near Pretoria, in the heart of Boer country, Rhodes and his partner Rudd go to buy a farm in the Transvaal as a new base for gold prospecting. While there Rhodes hears that Pickering has suffered a relapse and is gravely ill. Desperate to be at his side as quickly as possible, Rhodes travels the 300 miles to Kimberley on top of a mailcoach. Rhodes nurses his friend to the last. At his funeral, he is demented with grief.

The bereft Rhodes now ploughs all his energy into expanding his territory in search of gold. He has full ownership of the De Beers mine and sets his sights on the Kimberley mine, the majority of which is owned by his great rival, Barney Barnato.

Rhodes nurses the ailing Neville Pickering

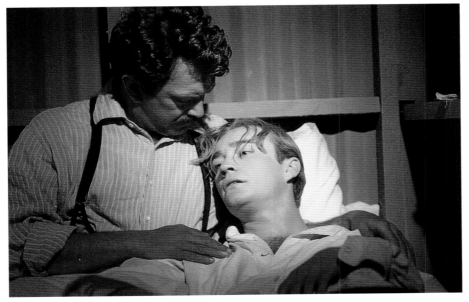

Rhodes *tackles the princess over the rumours she has been spreading that they are engaged to be married. He is furious but she still offers herself as his wife. Spurned, she now tackles Barney Barnato's nephew and business partner, Solly Joel, for his version of events…*

It's 1887 and Barney still controls the Kimberley mine – which Rhodes knows to be more valuable than his own, De Beers. Rhodes approaches Barney, offering him a directorship of De Beers, but Barney turns him down, convinced that he will outlast Rhodes. Rhodes desperately tries to increase his stake in the Kimberley mine, but in doing so he merely pushes up the value of Barney's shares. Rhodes offers Barney the chance to sell out at the high price, but still he refuses.

Rhodes has spent himself into a corner and announces a massive sale of diamonds to raise capital, knowing that only Barney can afford to buy. Barney can't believe his luck – if he buys, he'll flood the market and destroy his greatest rival, and if he refuses to buy, Rhodes is sunk anyway. Barney agrees to buy the diamonds at a fair price. As he signs, Rhodes tips the whole lot into a bucket. It will take six weeks to sort them again. Rhodes now has money and time to fight Barney. Barney can't fail to be impressed by this sting.

Rhodes now seriously woos Barney, offering to make him a life governor of De Beers in exchange for Barney's share of Kimberley and membership of the exclusive Kimberley Club, which is barred to Jews. At last Rhodes has found Barney's weak spot. He sells out to Rhodes. De Beers now owns 95 per cent of the world's diamond production. Rhodes, however, has far bigger ambitions. He approaches Frank Thompson, the manager of the De Beers compound, and tells him that he plans to expand north as far as the Zambezi. The territory is ruled by a wily old Zulu warrior, Lobengula, king of the Matabele. Rhodes wants exclusive mineral rights throughout his domains and plans to send Rudd, Thompson and Rochfort Maguire, his foppish lawyer friend from Oxford, to negotiate.

Barney objects to signing away money for these schemes – he's a businessman, not an emperor. Rhodes explains that if there are diamonds in Kimberley and gold in the Transvaal, more mineral wealth must lie beyond. He believes that Mashonaland is the site of King Solomon's Mine, the source of the riches of the Queen of Sheba. A generation ago, the Matabele conquered the territory and established their stronghold at Gubulawayo. A 'naked old savage', Lobengula, is all that stands between Rhodes and the biblical kingdom of Ophir.

Rhodes already has a letter from Sir Hercules Robinson, commending the mission to Lobengula on behalf of Queen Victoria. A network of missionaries throughout Africa will be their standard-bearers. He persuades Barney that if they don't take the land, other colonial powers will. All they have to do is secure the mineral rights and register them with the British Government. And, he asks, would Barney rather be remembered as someone who filled his own pockets, or as the founder of a new **country**?

Martin Shaw as Rhodes

Again, Barney gives in. Thompson, Rudd and Maguire enter Lobengula's territory without consent and arrive at Reverend Helm's mission church. They are arrested by Matabele warriors and taken to the king at Gubulawayo. They prostrate themselves before the king, give him gifts and ask for permission to dig for gold. But Maund and Colenbrander, two other prospectors from a rival company owned by Lord Gifford, already have the king's ear. Thompson is told that the king wants guns in exchange for a concession to dig — which would be directly defying the British Government. Helm reluctantly agrees to smuggle arms through British territory.

Lobengula holds a grand *indaba* and agrees to give Rhodes the right to dig, but not exclusive rights. He signs the concession, not realizing that he has been tricked into signing away all mineral rights in his land in exchange for guns.

Rhodes rashly publishes news of the concession in the *Cape Argus*, claiming, falsely, that Lobengula has granted him exclusive rights in his territory and is warning off other prospectors. When Maund and Colenbrander pass this news to the king he is furious and sends two of his most trusted *indunas* to England to ascertain whether Queen Victoria had really given her authority for Rhodes to press for the concession. Rhodes's scheme to outwit Lobengula may well have backfired.

Lobengula learns that the concession he signed was fraudulent

EPISODE FOUR: **THE PRICE OF MY BLOOD**

Once again, the princess visits Rhodes, warning him that if he refuses to accept her as an ally, he must face her as an enemy. Undaunted by his threats, she visits Harry Currey, who is now a supporter of Merriman and a bitter opponent of Rhodes. He was once very close to Rhodes — what brought about such a radical change? Harry goes back to the time when Rhodes promoted him from messenger boy to company secretary of his Gold Fields Company…

RHODES

Rhodes is deeply frustrated by his failure to secure the rights to all the mineral wealth in Lobengula's kingdom. The king's two most trusted *indunas* are on their way to England together with the white prospectors Maund and Colenbrander with a letter repudiating Rhodes's concession.

Rhodes fails in his initial attempt to bribe Maund into joining forces with him, but when Maund arrives in Cape Town he learns that Rhodes has bought out Lord Gifford, so they are now on the same side. Maund and Colenbrander are instructed to proceed to England with the *indunas*, as planned. Queen Victoria will only hear what they want her to hear, as they will be the interpreters.

Before Rhodes follows them to England he must honour his deal with Lobengula, thus strengthening his claim that the king signed the concession knowingly, in exchange for guns. He dispatches Dr Jameson to Gubulawayo to deliver the promised arms.

When Lobengula's deputation meets Queen Victoria they are unexpectedly joined by Selous, a veteran hunter who speaks fluent Matabele. Rhodes's scheme backfires as the Queen now hears Lobengula's grievance as he intended. She is charmed by the *indunas* and agrees that 'It is dangerous to place too much power in the hands of one man'. She makes it clear that Rhodes was acting without her authority and that she does not intend to grant a royal charter for his concession.

Lobengula's warriors wreak a terrible revenge on Reverend Helm

Rhodes and Harry arrive in London on a mission to rescue the situation. A royal charter will never be granted without the concession, which Lobengula will know is fraudulent as soon as his *indunas* return to Gubulawayo. Maund makes arrangements for the *indunas* to travel back to Cape Town – via Brazil. The journey will take six months.

This gives Rhodes time to secure support for a royal charter among politicians, journalists, the clergy and businessmen, using bribery and persuasion. Meanwhile, Thompson and Maguire are still holed up at Gubulawayo. Unable to tolerate the primitive conditions, Maguire deserts. Fearing that his base is crumbling, Rhodes writes to Thompson, reminding him of the reward to come when the royal charter is finally granted, but omitting to mention that his share has already been pledged to Lord Gifford. Harry is already beginning to disapprove of the way Rhodes conducts his affairs.

Sir Hercules Robinson, governor-general of Cape Colony, has been sacked for abusing his position to further his own interests. Back in England, Rhodes offers him a directorship of De Beers if he will back his campaign for a royal charter. Rhodes meets the British Prime Minister, Lord Salisbury, who offers support for the charter but warns of tough opposition from Lord Chamberlain and his South Africa Committee.

Before the committee, Rhodes pleads that his cause is not commercial self-interest but the betterment of humanity. Rhodes wins over Lord Salisbury and the Dukes of Abercorn and Fife by promising to make them directors of the new Chartered Company and to name towns after them. He gambles shrewdly that the British Government will never back out of a country with towns named after members of its aristocracy. With so much political support behind him he is finally granted the royal charter.

Too late, Lobengula's *indunas* return to Gubulawayo with the news that the concession was fraudulent. The king learns that he has given away the wealth of the Matabele. He wreaks a terrible revenge on the Reverend Helm and Thompson flees in fear of his life.

Rhodes returns to Kimberley and announces the launch of the Chartered Company to his delighted shareholders. Their celebrations are interrupted by the arrival of Frank Johnson, a young mercenary soldier who worked for Lord Gifford for 18 months and who claims that Rhodes has cheated him of his just reward. Rhodes is impressed by the young soldier and asks him how many men he would need to take Mashonaland. He is planning to form his own 'pioneer' army.

Rhodes persuades Jameson and Thompson to go back to Gubulawayo to ask Lobengula to give permission for his 'pioneers' to pass through Matabeleland en route to Mashonaland. He promises to make Jameson the first governor of Mashonaland.

Rhodes now tackles Selous, the veteran white hunter whose knowledge of the territory and African customs is second to none. Selous reminds Rhodes that Lobengula is occupying Mashonaland illegally, and therefore has no right to grant access to it. Even Selous, however, cannot refuse Rhodes's terms and he agrees to guide his army into Mashonaland.

In Gubulawayo, Jameson delights the ailing king by greeting him in his native tongue. Lobengula is in agony with gout and Jameson promises to relieve the pain. He uses morphine, knowing that before long he'll be addicted and unable to refuse him anything he asks.

EPISODE FIVE: **THE CHAMELEON AND THE FLY**

The princess continues her conversations with Harry Currey, asking him if he has actual proof of Rhodes's misdemeanours. Harry continues his story...

Now dependent on Dr Jameson's pain-killing morphine, Lobengula tells the doctor the story of the chameleon and the fly – how the chameleon disguises herself by changing colour until the fly is lured into her trap. 'England is the chameleon and I am the fly,' he says. Powerless to resist, he gives Jameson permission to lead Rhodes's 'pioneer' column through his country.

Sir Hercules Robinson has been replaced as governor-general by the less malleable Sir Henry Loch, who reluctantly appoints Rhodes as Prime Minister of Cape Colony, acknowledging that he has the support of all sides of the House and of every newspaper but warning him against corruption in his administration.

Frank Johnson
(Gavin Hood)
leads Rhodes's
'pioneer' army
into Matabeleland

In Kimberley, Rhodes inspects his new army. The 'pioneer' column sets off, led by Jameson, Johnson and Selous. As they approach Matabeleland, Lobengula calls for them to retreat, rightly believing them to be an army. When they refuse, Matabele warriors gather to attack at first light, but are frightened off by a huge searchlight which they believe to be witchcraft.

The 'pioneer' column enters Mashonaland, which Rhodes believes to be the source of the riches of the Queen of Sheba. They are at Mount Hamden, which Rhodes declares will be his new capital, Salisbury.

Sir Henry Loch gets wind of the fact that Rhodes's agents are now fanning out, taking more territory and running guns as far as the Congo and the African lakes. He warns Rhodes that he must honour Britain's treaties and international obligations, and that he is absolutely forbidden to encroach on the territories of other European powers.

The princess tells Harry that Rhodes was acting to advance the human race, that great individuals are not bound by the morals or beliefs of their time. Currey continues his story, describing Rhodes's furious reaction to news that he, Harry, was engaged to be married. His wife, Ethelreda, believes that this was a turning point in Rhodes's life. She claims that when Harry left Rhodes to marry, the fire went out of Rhodes, and that from that moment he allowed other people to fight his battles and make his decisions...

Rhodes visits Jameson's camp at Fort Salisbury. The dream appears to be over – there is no gold in Mashonaland. The gold is in Matabeleland and Lobengula is sitting on it, but Rhodes has been expressly forbidden by the British Government and the Cape Parliament to attack without a legitimate reason. If Jameson can find an excuse to attack, Rhodes will back him all the way. Meanwhile they must find a way to finance the administration of Mashonaland.

Rhodes approaches Barney Barnato for his agreement to finance the venture out of De Beers because the Chartered Company is broke. Barney is bitter because he's been left out of Rhodes's empire-building schemes, but he agrees to release the funds because he fears that Rhodes will spread the word that a 'little Yid' came between England and her glories in Africa.

The princess finds that she is being thrown out of her hotel in Cape Town. Alfred Beit, Rhodes's most trusted business partner, tells her that Rhodes is sending her packing. In desperation, she turns back to Merriman. She reminds him that he had remained a senior minister in Rhodes's Government, despite his awareness of bribery, corruption and extortion on a massive scale. So why then did he suddenly resign? Merriman replies, 'In one word — Matabeleland.'

Jameson and Johnson are desperate for an excuse to attack the Matabele. When Johnson finds that telegraph wires have been cut he goes to the nearest Shona village and demands 100 head of cattle as compensation. The Shona are a peaceful people, ruled over by the warring Matabele. The chief explains that he cannot give away cattle, as the herds belong to Lobengula. Johnson threatens him with war, and the cattle are delivered.

When Lobengula hears that his cattle have been given away he sends an army, an '*impi*', to massacre and plunder the Shona village, giving his word that no white man is to be harmed. Jameson sends word to Rhodes that innocent women and children are being murdered and Rhodes gives him permission to attack, in defence of the Shona. Taken unawares, the Matabele are slaughtered mercilessly.

Rhodes is rapidly running out of funds. He promises to pay his new army with land and loot from Lobengula's kingdom. Alfred Beit foresees a catastrophe and begs Rhodes to pay his men with cash. If one volunteer signs his pledge for payment in loot, there will be no turning back. He'll have to take Matabeleland. And if Rhodes provokes a war with Lobengula, the British Government and the whole world will be against him.

EPISODE SIX: LAND, GOLD AND LOOT

The princess continues talking with Merriman. He tells her that Rhodes always planned meticulously, but Jameson was the bull at the gate. They got away with some awful things...

Sir Henry Loch recognizes that Lobengula has taken every possible step to avoid war. He warns Rhodes that if Jameson attacks the Matabele without provocation, he will send Imperial forces to impose his own settlement. Jameson may only take defensive action if attacked.

Realizing that Lobengula will never make the first move, Jameson tricks a handful of his men into believing that they were attacked by a group of Matabele. He telegraphs the governor-general, who authorizes him to take whatever action he must to protect himself and his men. This is all Jameson needs.

The 'pioneer' army moves into Matabeleland, pitching camp in a river valley. The king assembles his *impis*, in preparation for war. At dawn, the Matabele warriors swarm over the high ridge, towards the pioneers' laager. Again and again, the Matabele attack but they are powerless with their spears against the might of the automatic Maxim guns. They are slaughtered in their hundreds.

Lobengula concedes defeat by razing Gubulawayo to the ground before fleeing north with his few remaining followers. The triumphant Jameson and his men march into the smouldering ruins, where young Johnny Grimmer raises the Chartered Company flag. Rhodes is not far behind. He has come to join the celebrations and inspect his new territory, which becomes known as 'Rhodesia'. Rhodes is just 41 years old but his health is failing. Time is running out.

Johnson and his men relentlessly pursue Lobengula to his forest camp. This time the Matabele warriors defend themselves with guns – guns supplied by Rhodes – but they are defeated. Lobengula, who by now is suffering from smallpox, bids farewell to his people, telling them Rhodes is now lord of his land as the lion is lord over the forest. His people should look to him for their protection. He then commits ritual suicide.

Rhodes returns to London and announces to his triumphant shareholders that the value of their shares in the Chartered Company has increased by 1500 per cent and that they own 'everything in Africa except the air'.

The princess presses Merriman for further information – Rhodes must be exposed and stopped. Merriman explains that it is too late, that once Rhodesia was founded he could do anything he wanted, including driving the natives into reserves so poor and overcrowded that they would be forced to sell their labour to the whites in order to survive. And if it worked in Rhodesia – why not in South Africa? The Boers would certainly support him...

In the Cape Parliament Rhodes makes a stirring speech, laying the foundations of apartheid by establishing the first permanent native reserves in Cape Colony.

Rhodes buys the services of the American engineering genius, John Hammond, recruiting him to take over all his gold-mining interests as chief engineer to the Chartered Company. Hammond tells him that Johannesburg sits on top of limitless wealth – but this territory is in the Transvaal, the Boer republic ruled over by the obstinate Paul Kruger.

Hammond advises Rhodes that there is no possibility of a second Johannesburg in Rhodesia. He urges Rhodes to take on Kruger and the Boers – all that stands between him and the wealth of Johannesburg. Rhodes wants to negotiate with Kruger but the relentless Jameson supports Hammond. He reminds Rhodes that he needs funds to fulfil his dream of expanding the British Empire from the Cape to Cairo. All Jameson needs is an excuse to attack Johannesburg.

There is already unrest in Johannesburg among the non-Dutch citizens, the *Uitlanders*, who are heavily taxed and denied the vote. Rhodes warns Kruger that if he continues to deny the people of Johannesburg the vote, they will be provoked to violence. Kruger says his people were led to the Transvaal by God. He will not subject them to the views of a foreign rabble who are only in Johannesburg to fill their pockets.

Rhodes now hatches a plot to provoke a rebellion among the mostly British *Uitlanders*, having first smuggled arms into the Transvaal through Bechuanaland. When the rebellion erupts, Jameson will be on the border, ready to respond to a call for help. But Johannesburg must make the first move. If Jameson moves first, it will be an unprovoked attack on a friendly state and Rhodes will have every colonial power in Europe against him.

Rhodes tells Beit that Jameson must have a base in Bechuanaland, that the press must be managed to secure public opinion and that Sir Henry Loch must go, to be replaced by Sir Hercules Robinson. Beit points out that Rhodes can't possibly have the power to replace the governor-general and, in any case, Sir Hercules is utterly discredited. He will never be reinstated...

Rhodes greets Sir Hercules and his wife on their return to Cape Town.

Frances Barber as Princess Radziwill

EPISODE SEVEN: **UPSETTING THE APPLE CART**

Rhodes continues to plot against Kruger and Johannesburg. In England, the Conservatives are back in power. Rhodes receives word that the new colonial secretary, his old adversary Joseph Chamberlain, will give him every assistance with his venture – provided that, officially, he knows nothing.

The princess now questions Dr Hans Sauer, a prominent Boer who was Rhodes's principal agent in the gold fields but who now ranks among Rhodes's sworn enemies. He tells her of telegrams between Chamberlain, Rhodes and Jameson which would prove their involvement in the conspiracy and which Rhodes would have kept to use against the British Government, in case they threatened to disown him.

Sir Hercules advises Rhodes that he is putting the Bechuanaland Police at his disposal and that a strip of land along the Transvaal border, supposedly for the construction of a railway line north, will be Jameson's base.

Rhodes instructs Jameson to go to Johannesburg to secure a letter, a passionate plea for help, from the men planning the *Uitlander* rebellion. The letter must be undated. When the rebellion erupts, he can insert the date and the letter will prove that he was merely responding to a cry for help. Jameson meets his fellow conspirators in the Rand Club to agree the wording of the letter. Barney Barnato's nephew, Solly Joel, is among them.

Kruger has heard that a force is gathering on his border and summons Barney Barnato, who has always treated the Boers with respect, to question him. Barney gives him his word that none of the directors of De Beers are involved in a conspiracy against him.

The *Times* correspondent of Johannesburg informs Rhodes that the conspirators plan to form a new republic following their rebellion. Rhodes advises him to inform the conspirators that he will insist on the Union Jack being raised in the Transvaal. Sir Hercules Robinson, the British Government and even the editor of *The Times* are all now heavily involved in Rhodes's secret plot to take Johannesburg.

Rhodes sends coded word to Jameson to commence action, but he is immediately warned that the conspirators are not ready for the revolt. Reluctantly, Rhodes heeds Beit's advice and wires Jameson instructing him to retreat. But Jameson is hell-bent on action, ignores the command and advances against Johannesburg. The panic-stricken Sir Hercules warns Rhodes that the British Government will disassociate itself from an act of war against a friendly state and that if Rhodes's involvement can be proved, his company's charter will be revoked.

Jameson and his men are routed by the Boers and the raid is a debacle. Fearing he has lost everything, the distraught Rhodes reveals his innermost feelings to his trusted private secretary, Philip (Flippy) Jourdan.

Four years later, the princess visits Flippy in hospital and convinces him that she is working to repair Rhodes's damaged reputation. She persuades him to hand over telegrams which will reveal the truth about the Jameson Raid.

The conspirators are arrested, including Barney's nephew, Solly. Barney is devastated at this betrayal. He goes to see Rhodes, who has announced his resignation as Prime Minister, to express his disgust. Barney will put pressure on Kruger to release Solly from prison by threatening to close down his mining operations in the Transvaal and bankrupting the country. As for the rest of the conspirators – their fate is in Rhodes's hands.

Jameson is informed that he will be deported and tried in Britain. Rhodes is summoned before Joseph Chamberlain, secretary of state for the Colonies, in London. Chamberlain is aware of the existence of telegrams and documents that would implicate the British Government in the Jameson Raid and invoke the wrath of other European powers. Rhodes points out that Chamberlain has denied the involvement of Her Majesty's Government before the House. He will accept personal responsibility for the raid as long as his company's charter for Rhodesia is secure.

Back in Rhodesia further trouble is brewing. The Matabele and Mashona unite in bloody rebellion against the European settlers. On his way back to Africa, Rhodes is informed that Barney has taken his own life.

Rhodes now resolves to solve the problems in his new country. Convinced that the natives want peace, Rhodes walks unarmed into the battlefield to negotiate with the Matabele leaders. They are prepared to surrender to Rhodes, on condition that he stays in the country to see that justice is done. He gives them his word that he will remain amongst them.

Hailed by the Matabele as their new leader, 'Ulodzi', Rhodes visits the tomb of Mzilikazi, founder of the Matabele nation, to appease his spirit. As the warriors roar their approval, he receives news that there is to be a full parliamentary enquiry into the Jameson Raid. He must return to England at once. Colenbrander reminds him that he has just given his word to the Matabele *indunas* that he will stay in Rhodesia. Rhodes retorts that if things go wrong in London, there will no longer be a Rhodesia…

Rhodes visits the tomb of Mzilikazi, founder of the Matabele nation

EPISODE EIGHT: THE RECKONING

It is 1897 and Rhodes is brought before the British Government's committee of inquiry, which is investigating the Jameson Raid. The radical MP Labouchère questions Rhodes closely. Rhodes explains that he placed a body of troops on the Bechuanaland border in his capacity as chairman of the Chartered Company, not as Prime Minister of the Cape. He denies emphatically the involvement of Sir Hercules Robinson, Joseph Chamberlain, Lord Gifford or the directors of De Beers in the plan to provoke insurrection in Johannesburg and he takes full personal responsibility for the debacle. He thus prevents the release of telegrams and documents that would reveal the extent of his corruption and misdemeanours in Africa.

He visits Jameson in prison to tell him of his plans to expand into Barotseland and to form a new party to fight in the next Cape elections. Jameson tells him that

it's all over, that he'll never win an election because he's lost the support of the Boers for ever. Rhodes is undaunted. His new party will be called the Progressive Party and he will win the support of the black population.

Jameson is released from prison and joins Rhodes on his campaign trail in the Malay quarter of Cape Town. There Rhodes sees his old manservant, Christmas, in the crowd. Rhodes makes a hopeless gesture of friendship towards his former companion, but Christmas refuses to acknowledge his former friend and master.

Rhodes campaigns to unite southern Africa under the British flag, from the Cape to the African lakes, exploiting the growing conflict between Briton and Boer with unashamedly anti-Boer speeches. When Merriman wins the election by a tiny majority in 1899, he visits Rhodes and asks him to use his influence in Britain to prevent war with Kruger becoming inevitable. When Rhodes refuses, Merriman asks him to consider what he's done in Africa. He's created a country where whites are divided against blacks, and against themselves.

The princess visits Rhodes at Groote Schuur. She now has the secret telegrams which could seriously compromise people in high positions in England and southern Africa. When Rhodes threatens to have her arrested for receiving stolen property, she points out that the documents would be the principal exhibit in a public trial. He tries to buy her off, but she is still obsessed with the idea of becoming his wife, a partner in his great enterprise. He brushes her attempt at blackmail aside. With a war on, no-one would publish anything injurious to the British Government. She points out that no-one has yet declared war...

Kruger receives an ultimatum from the British Government demanding that he disarms the Transvaal, grants home rule to Johannesburg and repeals every law passed in the last 18 years. It is, in effect, a declaration of war.

Rhodes returns to Kimberley which, along with other principal towns in the colony, is besieged by the Boers. Rhodes infuriates Colonel Kekewich, the British commanding officer, by criticizing his military operation and threatening to raise his own volunteer army with the arms and ammunition left over from the Jameson Raid. Kekewich orders Rhodes to leave town immediately. Kruger has sworn that if he captures Rhodes, he will parade him through the streets of Pretoria in a lion's cage.

Rhodes refuses to leave Kimberley, which is bombarded repeatedly by the Boers. His favourite 'pioneer' soldier, Johnny Grimmer, gets through enemy lines and brings news that the Boers are thrashing the British army throughout southern Africa. Rhodes is summoned to see Colonel Kekewich, who accuses him of sending messages through enemy lines and communicating with the British commander-in-chief directly. Kimberley is perfectly capable of defending itself without outside help he says, telling Rhodes there are more important issues in the war than whether De Beers is able to resume mining.

In her humble lodgings in Cape Town the princess is visited by Captain Widdowson, chief of the governor-general's Criminal Investigation Department. She is being investigated as a suspected enemy agent as she is known to associate with Boer sympathizers. If she hands over the stolen telegrams, however, charges will be dropped and her position in Cape Town will be restored. She tells him that the telegrams are lodged with the Russian consul, but that if he arrests her they could be subpoenaed as material evidence in a public trial. When Widdowson informs her that military offences aren't tried in public, she replies that, in that case, she will have to resort to crime.

To the fury of Colonel Kekewich, the interests of Rhodes do appear to override military concerns. Kimberley is relieved by General French after four months under siege and De Beers can resume its commercial operations.

The princess starts forging Rhodes's signature on promissory notes and guarantees, against which she is borrowing large sums of money. Rhodes learns of her activities and assures her that she is wasting her time – he will never allow her to play any part in his life. She claims that if she is charged with forgery and tried in public, he'll do anything to prevent the truth of his misdemeanours being revealed. He offers to pay her off, warning her that she'll destroy herself if she continues to flout the law. She replies that they will probably destroy each other.

Princess Radziwill relentlessly continues to forge Rhodes's signature, falsely acquiring larger and larger sums of money. Rhodes is prepared to let her continue, but Jameson urges him to bring charges of forgery – the telegrams will not be admitted as evidence in such a case. As usual, Beit counsels caution, but Jameson tips off the *Cape Argus* and the princess is exposed in a leading article. Rhodes now has no option but to prosecute.

The princess is arrested and charged with forgery. Owing to the ill-health of the chief witness, the case is adjourned but the princess refuses to accept the adjournment and insists that the trial is held at Groote Schuur – in Rhodes's bedroom if necessary.

Rhodes is now terminally ill. The heart condition that has afflicted him for all his 48 years now threatens his life. The trial is abandoned as Rhodes is taken to his cottage near the sea to die.

Denied her opportunity to expose Rhodes in public, the princess literally hounds him to the last, waiting in the crowd outside the cottage for news of his death.

On 26 March 1902, two months before the end of the Boer War, Rhodes dies, nursed to the end by Jameson and Johnny Grimmer. He is buried in his favourite place, the Matopos hills in the heart of Rhodesia, close to the tomb of Mzilikazi.

WHO'S WHO: *ALPHABETICAL GUIDE TO THE MAIN CHARACTERS*

ALFRED AYLWARD (Mark Drewry): an Ulsterman, rabble-rouser, racist, outlaw and Kimberley correspondent of the London *Daily Telegraph*.
BABAYANE (Ramolao Makhene): One of Lobengula's two most trusted councillors (*indunas*) who was sent to England to verify Rhodes's concession with Queen Victoria.

BARNEY BARNATO (Ken Stott): East-End Jew, amateur boxer and music-hall entertainer. He arrived in the diamond fields as a circus clown and magician but within a few years he had become Rhodes's most dangerous rival in the battle to monopolize the world's diamonds. Rhodes threw millions of pounds, as well as his immense resources of charm and cunning, into the fight to take over Barney's companies. In the end, Rhodes's De Beers Mining Company secured the monopoly, with Barney as its largest stockholder and a life director. The battle between the two men shifted to the newly discovered gold fields around Johannesburg, where both made a second vast fortune. He committed suicide in 1896.

ALFRED BEIT (Frantz Dobrowsky): a German Jew from Hamburg who made a fortune in the early days of Kimberley. He became a life director of De Beers and was one of Rhodes's most loyal friends and advisors. He never married and died in 1906, leaving the bulk of his vast fortune to charity.

JOSEPH CHAMBERLAIN (Oliver Cotton): formerly a radical member of the British Liberal Party and an opponent of Rhodes. Ultimately he became colonial secretary in Lord Salisbury's Conservative Government and secretly backed Rhodes's plot to take the Transvaal.

CHRISTMAS (Patrick Shai): manservant and friend to the young Rhodes when he first enters the diamond territory. He is the only fictional character in the series. He can be seen as a living symbol of countless thousands of black South Africans who were betrayed and broken by Rhodes but who earn no mention in history.

COLENBRANDER (Ian Roberts): an interpreter, formerly working for Lord Gifford's Bechuanaland Exploring Company which threatened Rhodes's ambitions in Africa. Later, one of Rhodes's agents.

JOHN CURREY (Paul Ditchfield): private secretary to Sir Richard Southey, the first British administrator of the diamond territory, which was renamed Kimberley.

HARRY CURREY (Gresby Nash): son of John Currey. Harry was 12 years old when Rhodes lodged with his parents in the early days of the Kimberley diamond diggings. Ten years later, Rhodes made him secretary of his Gold Fields Company, and his personal assistant after the death of Pickering. Harry was frequently appalled by Rhodes's politics but the friendship survived until Harry announced his plans to marry. Rhodes immediately ordered him out of the house. Harry subsequently entered the Cape Parliament as an ally of Merriman's, and an opponent of Rhodes. He died in 1945, aged 83.

LORD GIFFORD (Victor Melleney): formerly chairman of the Bechuanaland Exploring Company. Later a director of Rhodes's Chartered Company.

JACK 'JOHNNY' GRIMMER (Alex Ferns): a stableboy at De Beers when he first caught the attention of Cecil Rhodes. He volunteered to join Johnson's 'pioneer' column, but was refused because of his lack of military experience. Rhodes settled the matter with a payment of £500 to Johnson. After Harry Currey's dismissal, Rhodes invited Grimmer to work as his private secretary. Uncouth and barely literate, Grimmer became Rhodes's closest companion towards the end of his life. During the siege of

Kimberley, Grimmer broke through Boer lines to be at Rhodes's side. In the final weeks, he nursed Rhodes day and night, and was at his side when he died. He survived Rhodes by only three months.

JOHN HAMMOND (Todd Jensen): a Californian, the most brilliant mining engineer of his generation. Enticed to South Africa by Barney Barnato with an offer of £50,000 a year, he defected when Rhodes upped the offer to £75,000. Hammond convinced Rhodes that the fabulous gold fields around Johannesburg were unique, and he was the strongest advocate of a plan to seize the territory by force from the Transvaal Boers. When the scheme failed, Hammond was tried and imprisoned in Pretoria.

DR RUTHERFOORD HARRIS (Guy de Lancey): Rhodes's political agent.

THE REVEREND C.D. HELM (Timothy Walker): a missionary from the London Missionary Society, trusted by Lobengula. He witnessed Lobengula signing Rhodes's fraudulent concession and smuggled guns into Lobengula's territory in defiance of the British Government, in return for payment. Helm argued in favour of arming the Matabele on the grounds that 'the substitution of long-range rifles for the stabbing *assegai* would diminish the loss of life in Matabele raids and thus be a distinct gain to the cause of humanity'.

DR LEANDER STARR JAMESON (Neil Pearson): a brilliant surgeon whose loyalty, charm and personal courage made him an ideal accomplice in Rhodes's most dangerous schemes. When a smallpox epidemic threatened to close the Kimberley mines, it was Jameson who risked his career and reputation by assisting Rhodes with a cover-up. When Lobengula, king of the Matabele, blocked Rhodes's expansion into Central Africa, it was Jameson who commanded Rhodes's mercenaries in the eventual bloody campaign against the Matabele and administered the conquered territories on Rhodes's behalf. But success and power finally went to the doctor's head: it was Jameson who ultimately destroyed Rhodes's political career with a reckless attempt to seize Johannesburg after Rhodes had instructed him to abandon the plan. He was sentenced to 10 months in prison, but was released after eight months due to ill health. He died in 1917. In the first elections to be held after the Boer War, Jameson led Rhodes's Progressive Party to victory in the Cape and he served as Prime Minister from 1904–1908. He was created a baronet in 1911.

SOLLY JOEL (Nicky Rebelo): Barney Barnato's nephew and business partner who was disgraced when he became implicated in the disastrous Jameson Raid on Johannesburg.

FRANK JOHNSON (Gavin Hood): emigrated from England to South Africa at the age of 16 with £5.00 in his pocket and the promise of a job in a bank. He joined the Bechuanaland Border Police, and at the age of 20 paid for his discharge, so that he could prospect for gold in Bechuanaland and Matabeleland. Like many small-time prospectors, he was squeezed out by Rhodes, but unlike the others, he was determined to fight back, and travelled to Kimberley to confront the mining magnate. Johnson found himself invited into Rhodes's closest circle. Rhodes made Johnson the commanding officer of the 'pioneer' column that took Mashonaland.

PHILIP 'FLIPPY' JOURDAN (Jeremy Crutchley): a parliamentary messenger, later one of Rhodes's companions, who unwittingly betrayed Rhodes by handing over secret telegrams to Princess Radziwill.

COLONEL KEKEWICH (Peter Guiness): officer commanding the British garrison during the siege of Kimberley in the Boer War.

PAUL KRUGER (Carel Trichardt): President of the Boer republic of the Transvaal. He spent his political life fighting for his country's independence. Rhodes was his principal adversary in this struggle. He was finally defeated by the combined might of the British Empire and died in exile in Switzerland two years later in 1904.

HENRY LA BOUCHERE (Antony Thomas): a radical MP in the House of Commons and member of the South Africa Committee. He opposed Rhodes's expansionist activities in Africa and later questioned him during the enquiry into the Jameson Raid.

LOBENGULA (Washington Sixolo): king of the Matabele, the most powerful warrior nation in Africa, founded by his father, Mzilikazi. An absolute monarch, with the power of life and death over his subjects, he was nevertheless a man with the highest standards of honour. When Rhodes's agents talked him into signing away the mineral rights of his country, he sent two of his principal *indunas* on the 6000-mile journey to England to plead the justice of his cause before Queen Victoria. Three years later, when Rhodes's mercenaries invaded his country, he granted his royal protection to the white traders and hunters residing in his capital. He committed suicide in 1894 after the defeat of his armies and was buried with full military honours.

SIR HENRY LOCH (Rex Garner): high commissioner and governor of Cape Colony. Successor to the corrupt Sir Hercules Robinson.

LOTSHE (Sam Williams): one of Lobengula's principal *indunas*. Lobengula blamed Lotshe for misleading him over the true nature of the concession he signed, which led to the loss of his kingdom to Rhodes. Lotshe was subsequently put to death by order of the king.

ROCHFORT MAGUIRE (Richard Huw): a lawyer and friend of Rhodes from Oxford. Responsible with Rudd and Thompson for securing a fraudulent concession from Lobengula. Ultimately he became a director of Rhodes's Chartered Company.

MAKWEKWE (Moshoeshoe Chabeli): A principal *induna* who committed suicide alongside Lobengula.

MAUND (Ron Smerczak): agent originally acting for Lord Gifford.

JOHN MERRIMAN (Philip Godowa): an incorruptible politician and champion of the rights of black workers. He befriended Rhodes in his early days and encouraged him to enter politics. At first he refused to believe the mounting evidence of his friend's ruthlessness and corruption. When the break finally came, Merriman prophesied an appalling future for South Africa if Rhodes's political ambitions were realized. He succeeded Jameson as prime minister of the Cape and was considered the only candidate for the premiership of the new South African nation established by the Act of Union in 1910 acceptable to the black population as well as the Boers, but was passed over by Gladstone.

MSHETE (Ken Gampu): One of Lobengula's two most trusted *indunas* who were sent to England to verify Rhodes's concession with Queen Victoria.

NEVILLE PICKERING (Ray Coulthard): a trainee clerk who was sent to Kimberley at the age of 20. He attracted the attention of Cecil Rhodes and was soon made secretary of the De Beers Mining Company. Within a year, Rhodes had willed his entire vast fortune to the young man with whom he shared his home. Pickering developed septicaemia after a riding accident and Rhodes immediately abandoned the newly discovered Johannesburg gold fields, travelling 300 miles on the roof of a mailcoach to be at his side. When Pickering died, Rhodes was demented with grief. After the funeral, no-one was permitted to mention Pickering's name again.

PRINCESS CATHERINE RADZIWILL (Frances Barber): a striking Russian aristocrat. Exiled from the Berlin court and estranged from her husband, she met Rhodes in London when he was at the height of his power, and, without doubt, the most eligible bachelor in the world. She followed Rhodes to Cape Town and charmed her way into his inner circle, where she began to delve into his personal and political life in an attempt to blackmail him into marriage. When she was rejected, the princess devised an ingenious revenge which hastened Rhodes's death and brought her public humiliation and imprisonment. She died in New York in 1941, aged 84.

SIR HERCULES ROBINSON (John Carson): high commissioner and governor-general of Cape Colony; dismissed for his corrupt association with Rhodes. He was later reinstated as a result of Rhodes's influence.

CHARLES RUDD (David Butler): Rhodes's first partner on the diggings. He later became a life director of De Beers.

LORD SALISBURY (Michael Atkinson): British Prime Minister from 1886–1892 and again from 1895–1902.

DR HANS SAUER (Paul Eilers): a Boer, and Rhodes's principal agent in the gold fields until the Jameson Raid, when he became a dangerous adversary.

FREDERICK SELOUS (Paul Slabolepszy): internationally renowned explorer, hunter and author. He was a leading authority on Africa and was persuaded by Rhodes to lead his 'pioneer' army north into Mashonaland.

SIDNEY SHIPPARD (Michael Richard): attorney-general of the diamond territory.

SOMABHULANA (Mawonga Tyawa): One of Lobengula's principal *indunas* who later negotiated peace with Rhodes on behalf of the Matabele.

SIR RICHARD SOUTHEY (John Rogers): the first British administrator of the diamond territory.

GORDON LE SUEUR (André Odendaal): a parliamentary messenger, later Rhodes's private secretary.

FRANK THOMPSON (Sean Taylor): De Beers compound manager. Fluent in five native languages, he later became Rhodes's principal agent in Matabeleland.

UMGANDANA (Vusi Kenene): Lobengula's crown prince, and a member of his royal guard. Umgandana was shot down when Jameson's men carried out a surprise attack on the Matabele.

UNGUBA (Jerry Mofokeng): one of Lobengula's principal *indunas*.

Chapter 14

South Africa and Zimbabwe – Then to Now

Long before the arrival of the white man in southern Africa, bands of nomadic hunter-gatherers roamed its great open spaces. About 2000 years ago some of these groups were introduced to the concept of property ownership and territory by the Sudanic peoples of the north. These groups were the first southern Africans to come into contact with the European seafarers of the sixteenth century.

Meanwhile people of a quite different culture occupied parts of what is now Zimbabwe. The wealthy Shona kept cattle and used iron. By the seventeenth century another powerful group, the Xhosa, had advanced as far south as the eastern Cape and were on a direct collision course with the European colonists.

The Dutch first established a permanent presence on the southern tip of Africa in 1652 as a station for the Dutch East India Company's passing fleets. The Cape outpost expanded steadily as trekboers and farmers took their sheep and cattle and moved into the hinterland. They soon came into conflict with the Xhosa and competition for grazing land inevitably led to confrontation. In 1779 the first of nine bloody frontier wars erupted.

By the end of the eighteenth century the power of the Netherlands was in decline and in 1806 the British took over at the Cape, which they were to govern for the rest of the century. For a time it seemed that borders could be agreed and that the Xhosa would be left in peace, but eventually the settlers resumed their push for territory and the black clans were progressively subdued.

Meanwhile, British hunters and traders began to settle in Port Natal (now Durban). Their arrival coincided with the meteoric rise to power of the astute warrior chief Shaka, who formed the Zulu nation in 1818, in a maelstrom of violence and counter-violence that engulfed the east coast and much of the interior. A group of Zulus led by Mzilikazi headed north and became known as the Ndebele (Matabele), settling in the west of what is now Zimbabwe in 1837, ruling over the more passive people of Mashonaland.

During the 1830s Boer trekkers (Afrikaners) rolled in to Port Natal from the west and came into conflict with Shaka's successor, Dingane, whom they finally defeated at Blood river in 1838. But it was the British who eventually prevailed – over both trekker and Zulu. The Boers were eased out of the fledgling colony of Natal in 1843 and the Zulus were crushed at Ulundi in 1879.

Many Dutch-speaking Cape settlers, disenchanted with the British authorities at the Cape and incensed by the abolition of slavery in 1834, had begun to head into the interior in a mass migration known as the Great Trek. The Boer exodus gathered momentum and eventually they controlled much of the territory north of the Orange river. By the 1850s their settlements were strong enough to warrant the creation of two independent Boer republics: the Orange Free State and the Transvaal.

The discovery of the fabulous Kimberley diamond fields at the end of the 1860s and the Witwatersrand golden reef 25 years later destroyed any chance of lasting peace between Boer and Briton. The northern region of the Boer-dominated Transvaal was fast becoming a prize worth fighting for.

The British imperialist Cecil Rhodes was convinced that even greater mineral wealth lay in the area north of the Transvaal, between the Limpopo and the Zambezi rivers. These territories, Mashonaland and Matabeleland, were dominated by the mighty Matabele king, Lobengula. In 1889 Rhodes tricked Lobengula into signing away the mineral wealth of Mashonaland, and in 1893, his newly-formed 'pioneer' army, led by Dr Jameson, invaded Matabeleland. The defeated king committed ritual suicide and, in 1894, Mashonaland and Matabeleland were renamed Rhodesia. Rhodes declared Salisbury his new capital and his Chartered Company controlled the new country until 1923.

The children of Soweto are the future of modern South Africa

The conflict between Boer and Briton in the Transvaal finally erupted in the Boer War (1899–1902), which left a legacy of bitterness, but the victorious British wanted reconciliation and on 31 May 1910 the Transvaal and the Orange Free State were united with the British colonies of the Cape and Natal to become provinces of the new Union of South Africa. Black Africans were not consulted in the creation of the unified state, and had no democratic rights within the new order.

The years between 1910 and 1948 saw South Africa's transformation into a powerful, modern industrial nation. They were years of profound social change – and of a growing racial divide.

The First World War stimulated the growth of urban areas. Tens of thousands of blacks – forced off the land by cattle disease, mechanization and drought – gathered around the cities in huge strictly controlled locations, with poor whites (mostly Afrikaners who couldn't compete with cheap African labour) on the fringes.

Conflict was inevitable. Economic depression, strikes and unrest were regular features of the interwar years. In this tense climate, successive Union governments pushed through new racial measures ranging from job reservation and urban segregation to the formal allocation of land to confine the rural Africans. These moves failed to satisfy the hard-liners and in 1948 the extremist Reunited National Party was elected to office to form South Africa's first all-Afrikaner Government.

Although the Nationalists of the 1950s and 1960s did not invent apartheid, they tied together the existing threads of racial prejudice to create one of the most all-embracing bodies of restrictive laws ever devised.

The Group Areas Act of 1950 segregated still further the country's cities and towns. Other laws involved racially-based identity documents (the so-called Pass Laws), the classification of people according to colour, segregation of amenities, and the prohibition of mixed marriage and sex across the colour line.

The black opposition, particularly the African National Congress, had its roots in the disillusionment that set in after the Boer War. For the next half-century, the ANC remained committed to a moderate stance which failed to advance the cause. The Sharpeville massacre in 1960, when 69 demonstrators were gunned down by police, was a turning point in the country's affairs. South Africa was expelled from the Commonwealth and faced isolation abroad and mounting racial conflict at home. The ANC launched its armed struggle, which led to the arrest of Nelson Mandela and other prominent ANC figures in 1963. They were sentenced to life imprisonment and consigned to Robben Island, to the west of Cape Town's shores.

Rhodesia, the country created by Rhodes, now under the leadership of Ian Smith, declared unilateral independence (UDI) from Britain in 1965. In 1980, after 14 years of bloody warfare, free elections were held. Ninety years after Rhodes's pioneer waggons first rolled into the territory, the Shona and Ndebele finally achieved independence. Robert Mugabe became prime minister and on 17 April 1980 the British flag was run down for the last time.

T H E   M A K I N G   O F   R H O D E S

In South Africa the struggle continued. P. W. Botha (prime minister 1978–1990) tried to stem the tide with a limited programme of domestic reform but the troubled years of his premiership brought a pattern of riots and unrest and draconian police reaction. By the late 1980s, the townships were in a state of anarchy and even conservative whites realized that they could no longer hold on to power.

When the ailing P. W. Botha was ousted in favour of F. W. De Klerk, the changes that followed were rapid, fundamental and dramatic. At the opening session of parliament in 1990, he announced the unbanning of the ANC. Two weeks later, Nelson Mandela, prisoner for the past 27 years, walked to freedom.

In 1994 South Africa's first democratic elections were held and Nelson Mandela was inaugurated as president of the Republic of South Africa on 10 May. He is the first head of state not to reside at Groote Schuur, the home that Rhodes created for himself at the foot of Table Mountain.

Nelson Mandela's presidency of South Africa marks the beginning of the end of the Rhodes era

On his death in 1902, Rhodes left the greater part of his vast fortune (valued in 1907 at £3 345 000) to the establishment of scholarships to study at Oxford University. Rhodes decreed that the scholarships were to be awarded to young men with regard to '(i) his literary and scholastic attainments (ii) his fondness of and success in manly outdoor sports (iii) his qualities of manhood, truth, courage, devotion to duty, sympathy for the protection of the weak, kindliness, unselfishness and fellowship, and (iii) his exhibition during school days of moral force of character and of instincts to lead and take an interest in his schoolmates, for those latter attributes will be likely in afterlife to guide him to esteem the performance of public duties as his highest aim.'

His original will provided for fifty-two scholarships each year. Twenty were for students from countries which then formed part of the British Empire (Canada, Australia, South Africa, Rhodesia, New Zealand, Newfoundland, Bermuda and Jamaica), with thrty-two for the United States of America. In a codicil to his will, Rhodes added five for Germany, on receipt of the news that the German Emperor had made instruction in English compulsory in German schools.

In 1977, Parliament extended eligibility to women, and the scheme, which has since also been extended to students from India, Pakistan, Nigeria, Singapore, Malaysia, Kenya, Hong Kong and the European Community, now makes ninety-four annual awards. To date, some 5 300 Rhodes Scholarships have been awarded to students who include Edward de Bono, Bob Hawke, Kris Kristofferson, Bryan Gould and Bill Clinton.

Rhodes House was built in Oxford in 1928 as a central headquarters for the Rhodes Scholarship scheme. The trustees named rooms in the building after Rhodes's friends, including Sir Leander Starr Jameson and Alfred Beit. Along the parapet of the south front are carved the words DOMUS HAEC NOMEN ET EXEMPLUM CECILI IOHANNIS RHODES OXONIAE QUAM DELIXIT IN PERPETUUM COMMENDAT which can be translated: 'This house stands forever as a reminder to the Oxford he loved of the name and example of Cecil Rhodes'.

Acknowledgements

The following people worked on the production of *Rhodes*:

Producers: Charles Salmon, Scott Meek
Director: David Drury
Creator and writer: Antony Thomas
Production Executive: Chris Catterall

Production Department
Production Supervisor: Pierre de C. Hinch
Production Co-ordinator: Carole W. Beresford
London Co-ordinator: Hermione Ninnim
Producer's Assistant: Romy B. Schumann
Production Secretary: Adi Hutchison Cook
Receptionist: Xoliswa Sithole
Production Assistants: Shane Markram, Lee Mardghum
Office Trainee: Klaas Hlungwani

Accounts Department
Chief Accountant: Barbara Bergman
First Assistant Accountant: Heather Sisson
Second Assistant Accountants: Sarah Bergman, Archana Casson, Trish Billinge

Casting Department
Casting Director (UK): Sarah Bird
Casting Director (SA): Christa Schamburger
Casting Assistants: Robin Charteris, Kerstin Eser
Stand-in for Martin Shaw: John Reynders
Stand-in: Arryn Eldon
Translator/Language Advisor: Victoria Blanchard

Assistant Directors
First Assistant Director: John Watson
Second Assistant Directors: Robert Quinn, Adam Browne
Third Assistant Directors: Lance Samuels, Philip Mosoeu
Floor Runner: Ben Drury
Matabele Co-ordinators: Bobby Duffas, Barry Leitch
Director's Driver: Roddy Gubese

Camera Department
Director of Photography: Alec Curtis
First Camera Assistant: Paul Langridge
Focus Pullers: Richard Palmer, Bernd Köter
Clapper Loaders: Abednigo Malinga, Amelia Henning, Gideon Furst, Marelize Pretorius

Second Unit Camera Department
Camera Operator: Digby Young
Focus Pullers: Werner Maritz, Glen Donaldson
Clapper Loader/Grip: Steven Ndo

Sound Department
Sound Mixer: Rüdiger Payrhuber
Boomswinger: Jonathon Kvalsvig
Trainee Sound: Bongani Tshabalala

Continuity Department
Continuity: Maureen Conway
Trainee Continuity: Nkosana Mntambo

Lighting Department
Gaffer: Bruce Thomas
Best Boy: Grant Forbes
Sparks: Mohammed Jali, Joseph Themba
Standby Sparks: Danny Smart, Clint Stone

Grips Department
Key Grip: J.P. Ridgeway
Assistant Grips: Rachimo Chokoe, Leonard Tsadeni, Mark Rowlston

Unit Department
Location Manager: Clive Stafford
Set Unit Manager: Walter Ayres
Unit Medic: John Schmit
Location Scouts: John Sleigh, Gerard Savineje
Senior Unit Assistant: T.J. Ngoepe
Unit Assistants: Richard Cathro, Gus Green, Tinus Drinkwater, Jan van Niekerk
Caterers: Mike/Andrew
Craft Service: Rosie

Transport Department
Transport Manager: Morgan Pather
Transport Captain: Jean Roux Viljoen

Wardrobe Department
Costume Designer: Lyn Avery
UK Wardrobe Assistants: Flora Avery, Morgan Elliot
Wardrobe Supervisor: Jeni Halliday
Wardrobe Assistants: Clinton Booyse,
    Catherine Fairley, Zureta Schulz, Georgia Kinghorn
Standby Wardrobe: Julie Palmer
Seamstresses: Aggrineth Mokwena, Vuyelwa Shabalala

Make-Up Department
Chief Make-Up/Hair: RoseAnn Samuel
First Assistant Make-Up/Hair: Gill Rees
Second Assistant Make-Up/Hair: Elaine Nicholas Browne
Hair and Make-Up Dailies: Elaine de Lange,
    Mary Reid, Sue Michaels

Art Department
Production Designer: Maurice Cain
Supervising Art Directors: Ben Scott, Justin
    Warburton-Brown
Art Director: Zack Grobler
Assistant Art Director: Claude van Bavel
Art Department Co-ordinator: Loreley Yeowart
Researcher: Gail Behrman
Waggon Co-ordinator: Rod Black
Waggon Supplier: Dawie van Heerden
Scenic Artist: Roland Hunter
Graphic Artist: Rae Wynne Roberts

Props Department
Production Buyer: Peter Rutherford
Assistant to the Production Buyer: Julie Robertson
Assistant Props Buyer: Jeanne Henn
Props Master: Dirk Buchman
Set Dressers: Tony Mexter, Bob Toms, Wayne Newton
Standby Props: Elias Remaila
Props Storeman: Eran Singh
Props Driver: Willy Smith

Construction Department
Construction Co-ordinator: Mary Da Silva
Foreman: Joel Van Bavel
Carpenters: Willem Schimmel, Matt Buenzli, Hennie
    Goddard, Gregory Roux, Antony Van Rensburg,
    Gary Brown, Sean Ahern
Construction (Lobengula's kraal): Barry Leitch
Standby Carpenter: Cedric Chetty

Stunt Department
UK Stunt Co-ordinator: Gerry Crampton
SA Stunt Co-ordinator: Gavin Mey
Horse Master: Rick Snowdon
Horse Department Co-ordinator: Carol Mey
Riding Instructor: Mike Oosthuizen
Stuntmen: Don Reid, Brian Jenkins, Tay Lucey,
    Philip Notununo, Lance Ceronio

Special Effects Co-Ordinator
UK SFX Co-ordinator: Ken Lailey
SA SFX Co-ordinator: Max Poolman
Armourers: Jacques Hoffman, Bruce Wentzel

Drivers
Artist Drivers: Alpheus Manaka, Thekiso Maletsane,
    Philip Notununo, Oupa Mandiwana
Unit Truck: Enoch Mokoto
Unit Genny: Harry Malema
Camera Truck: Jacob Mothiba
Lighting Truck: Pepsi Mahuwisi
Grips Truck: William Magota
'Priscilla': Wilson Shamba
Wardrobe Truck: Vernon Gumede
M.C.C. Genny: Peter Makwela

Publicity Department
UK Publicity: Fliss Coombs
SA Publicity: Dezi Rörich, Dave Wilson
Stills Photographers: Umberto Adaggi, Lisa Trocchi

Music Department
Music Producer: Graham Walker
Music Co-ordinator: Liz Schrek
Composer: Alan Parker

Post-Production Department
Post-Production Supervisor: Mike Nunn
Post-Production Co-ordinator: Harriet Salmon
Editor: Ian Farr
Assistant Editor: Thomas Ash
Second Assistant Editor: Jackie Ophir
Sound Editors: Nigel Galt, Mike Redbourne,
    Paul Conway, Richard Settes
ADR Mixers: Brian Saunders, Mike Dowson